W9-DAQ-868

The Welles - Turner Memorial Library
Glastonbury, Connecticut

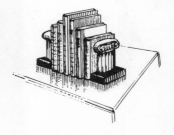

Accession No. _____

SHERLOCK HOLMES
AND HIS CREATOR

BY THE SAME AUTHOR

*Old Conjuring Books: A Bibliographical and
Historical Study with a Supplementary Check-List*

The Late Mr. Sherlock Holmes

SHERLOCK HOLMES
AND
HIS CREATOR

TREVOR H. HALL

with contributions by
Archdeacon Charles O. Ellison

ST. MARTIN'S PRESS
NEW YORK

Printed in Great Britain
Library of Congress Catalog Card Number: 77-18322
First published in the United States of America in 1978

Library of Congress Cataloging in Publication Data

Hall, Trevor H.
 Sherlock Holmes and his creator.

 Includes indexes.
 1. Doyle, Arthur Conan, Sir, 1859-1930—Characters—
Sherlock Holmes—Addresses, essays, lectures.
I. Ellison, Charles O. II. Title.
PR4624.H255 823'.9'12 77-18322
ISBN 0-312-71718-0

12/78

CONTENTS

ABBREVIATIONS

THE CANON

S.   *The Complete Sherlock Holmes Short Stories* (London, 1928)

L.   *The Complete Sherlock Holmes Long Stories* (London, 1929)

GENERAL REFERENCES

Carr   John Dickson Carr, *The Life of Sir Arthur Conan Doyle* (London, 1949)

Hall (I)   *Sherlock Holmes. Ten Literary Studies* (London & New York, 1969)

Hall (II)   *The Late Mr. Sherlock Holmes* (London & New York, 1971)

Lamond   Rev. John Lamond, *Arthur Conan Doyle. A Memoir* (London, 1931)

Memories   Sir Arthur Conan Doyle, *Memories and Adventures* (London, 1924)

Nordon   Pierre Nordon, *Conan Doyle* (London, 1966)

Pearson   Hesketh Pearson, *Conan Doyle. His Life and Art* (London, 1943)

PREFACE

I HOPE that admirers of Sir Arthur Conan Doyle and lovers of Sherlock Holmes may find something of interest in this collection of essays. My earlier books about the world's greatest of all fictional detectives were wholly exercises in the "Higher Criticism" of the literature of Baker Street, an amusing formula briefly originated by Frank Sidgwick over seventy years ago,[1] to be developed by Andrew Lang in 1904[2] and Ronald Knox in 1912[3] and by many other distinguished writers during the intervening years. The late Dorothy L. Sayers observed that "the rule of the game is that it must be played as solemnly as a county cricket match at Lords".[4] I agree, with the qualification that this kind of pseudo-scholarship is, in my experience, capable of being misunderstood by the uninitiated.

In October, 1971, I was invited to speak on a literary subject of my own choice to the staff and post-graduate students of the School of English in the University of Leeds. It was an amusing and revealing afternoon. In the opening part of the lecture I endeavoured to explain something of the history and purpose of the Higher Criticism of Sherlock Holmes, inevitably quoting from the work of other writers and my own books in so doing. Despite this fair warning, I discovered that my solemn and evidently persuasive "bibliographical scrutiny of Holmes's own literary output", dressed up as it was by mischievous references to *The English Catalogue*, *The British Museum*

---

[1] "An Open Letter to Dr. Watson", *The Cambridge Review*, 23 January, 1902, concerning *The Hound of the Baskervilles*.
[2] "At the Sign of the Ship", *Longman's Magazine*, July, 1904, on the subject of *The Three Students*. In an essay on Conan Doyle published in the same month in *The Quarterly Review*, Lang also amusingly applied the Higher Criticism to *The Sign of Four* and *The Noble Bachelor*.
[3] "Studies in the Literature of Sherlock Holmes", first published in *The Oxford Blue Book* in 1912 and afterwards reprinted in *Essays in Satire* in 1928.
[4] *Unpopular Opinions* (London, 1946), p. 7.

Catalogue and Bertram Dobell's *Catalogue of Books Printed for Private Circulation*, was evidently being accepted by some of my learned audience as a serious literary study. The academic leg is easily pulled, it would seem, even when the conjurer reveals the secret of the trick prior to its performance.

The present collection differs to some extent from my previous work in this field, and this variation becomes more marked towards the end of the book. First, however, and most importantly, it is a great pleasure to me that my friend Archdeacon Charles O. Ellison has contributed two chapters. As both his degree and his early training were in chemistry, he is ideally qualified to write about Holmes's most important hobby. As Archdeacon Ellison was born in Leeds, it is also highly appropriate that he should be the first Sherlockian scholar to examine the topographical aspects of Holmes's tantalising reference to the *Leeds Mercury* in *The Hound of the Baskervilles*.

Both Charles Ellison's essays are pure exercises in the "Higher Criticism" of the Sherlock Holmes stories, as is my own chapter on the life of Moriarty. The chapter on Holmes and Sigmund Freud, still in the same category, is a documented correction of a violation of the canon at one of its most significant periods, that of *The Final Problem* and the relations between Holmes and Moriarty in April, 1891. The credibility to a fundamentalist like myself of the notion published by Mr. Nicholas Meyer that Moriarty, "the Napoleon of crime", was merely a cocaine-induced delusion on the part of the world's greatest detective can be compared with that of an essay, "Watson was a Woman", contributed by Rex Stout to the collection *Profile by Gaslight*, edited by Edgar W. Smith and published in New York in 1944. In this investigation, I am indebted to my friend Percy H. Muir for much help, just as was the late Harold W. Bell, the author of *Sherlock Holmes and Dr. Watson. The Chronology of their Adventures* (London, 1932). In this now extremely rare book, one of the earliest examples of the "Higher Criticism", Bell wrote over forty years ago, "Mr. Percy H. Muir has sent me encouragement, and valuable information for dating *Thor Bridge*". The presentation copy signed "For Percy H. Muir, with much gratitude. H. W. Bell.

6.x.32", and re-inscribed as a gift to me in 1974, is a treasured item on my shelves.

The two chapters on the interaction of the work of T. S. Eliot and Maurice Leblanc with the Sherlock Holmes stories contain some elements of the Higher Criticism, but they do nevertheless come into the category of genuine, if light-hearted, exercises in literary inquiry. I am not the first student to point out the use that the late T. S. Eliot made of the Baker Street canon in some of his poems, but I hope that I am the first writer to assemble all the facts in permanent form. So far as I am aware, I have broken new ground in the study of those of Maurice Leblanc's stories that describe the rivalry between Sherlock Holmes and Arsène Lupin. I think it true to say that this chapter would not have been attempted had I not read T. S. Eliot's remark in *The Criterion* in 1929 that he himself hoped to write at length on the subject, followed by my failure to discover any trace of his having implemented such an excellent intention. "The Origin of Sherlock Holmes" is a serious attempt to bring together for comparison the conflicting theories in regard to the circumstances that led to that historic moment in Southsea in 1886 when Dr. A. Conan Doyle sat down to write *A Study in Scarlet*. I am indebted to Ellery Queen for his personal kindness to me in stimulating this exercise.

The essay, "Conan Doyle and Spiritualism", which is by far the longest, tries to offer a solution to a question that has puzzled me for many years. It is possible that the original seed of the problem was sown in my mind when long ago, my late father, Harold Roxby Hall, introduced me to Sir Arthur Conan Doyle. After an hour in his company among his psychic exhibits it is understandable that a schoolboy like myself was nearly converted to spiritualism then and there. Thirteen years ago I wrote of this incident:

> "I have been a Sherlock Holmes enthusiast since my schooldays and it was as a schoolboy that my father, who was acquainted with Sir Arthur Conan Doyle, introduced me to the creator of my hero. The meeting took place in Sir Arthur's psychic bookshop in Westminster, and we were invited to inspect the curious exhibits in the basement museum. The impression made upon a small boy

by the greatest exponent and champion of spiritualism in its history was clearly formidable, and my father, who was a wise man, decided that an immediate antidote was necessary. We went to Maskelyne's, where I saw that greater miracles than those described by Sir Arthur could be accomplished in full light by normal means. An enthusiasm for amateur conjuring was a natural development".[1]

I was thus headed away from spiritualism at an early age by the awakening of my interest in the secrets of conjuring. Subsequent experience in critical psychical research, including an examination of the notorious case of Borley Rectory and some other outstanding examples of fraud and gullibility in the history of spiritualism, has made me a fairly hardened sceptic in regard to the subject in which Doyle wholeheartedly believed, and to which he enthusiastically devoted the last fourteen years of his life. To me, a life-long admirer of Sir Arthur Conan Doyle as a man and a writer, the situation was a puzzle, to which I thought it conceivable I might bring some sort of balanced view.

My indebtedness to the published work of many of the writers who have preceded me is acknowledged in the text. Other authors and commentators from whose writings I have profited include Evelyn Herzog, Constance Nicholas, R. M. Fleisner, G. W. Hallam, W. D. Jenkins, H. W. Starr and H. T. Webster. I am grateful to Messrs. John Murray, the publishers of almost the whole of the literature of Sherlock Holmes and Conan Doyle, for permission to quote from the many books contained in my collection bearing the imprint of that distinguished firm. My obligation to the late Adrian Conan Doyle, who gave me permission to write about Sherlock Holmes and to quote from the stories, remains undiminished. He was kind enough to say that from his point of view the fact that I had met his father made me one of "the inner circle". I gratefully extend this expression of indebtedness to Baskerville Investments Ltd.

My warm thanks are due to my friend Alan H. Wesencraft, the Reference Librarian of the University of London Library, who made available to me from the press-cuttings books in his care much valuable information about Sir Arthur Conan Doyle.

[1] "A Magical Library", *Journal* of the Private Libraries Association, July, 1963. The paragraph was quoted in the Introduction to my *New Light on Old Ghosts* (London, 1965).

I am indebted to Lady (Pauline) Joy, who gave me considerable assistance in regard to the many unpublished letters from Doyle to Sir Oliver Lodge, and to my secretary, Mrs. Susan Spriggs, for her care in preparing the typescript. The documentation of the final chapter would have been noticeably the poorer had it not been for the kindness of my friend and colleague of many years, Dr. Eric J. Dingwall, who placed his large library of books on psychical research at my disposal at his home in Sussex.

T. H. H.

Thorner, Yorkshire.
August, 1976.

I

DR. JAMES MORIARTY

IN the annals of criminology, studies of men of outstanding intellectual power who have devoted their gifts to the organisation of crime on a vast scale,[1] such as Fritz Lang's Dr. Mabuse and Sax Rohmer's Dr. Fu-Manchu, have always been of paramount and absorbing interest. It is therefore unfortunate that a biography of the even more sinister "ex-Professor Moriarty of mathematical celebrity",[2] referred to by Sherlock Holmes as "the Napoleon of crime"[3] and by Dr. Watson as "a man whose record was black with unutterable infamies",[4] should so far not have been attempted.

It is true that a most distinguished Sherlockian, the late Edgar W. Smith, published his pamphlet, *The Napoleon of Crime* in 1953.[5] He modestly, and indeed truthfully, described it as "a trifling monograph",[6] for it consisted of only a few pages. It did not claim to be a biographical study, and was more concerned to throw light on some relevant aspects of the history of physics. Smith suggested, for example, that "it is impossible to escape the conclusion that Moriarty, long before Albert Einstein, glimpsed the awful potentialities of the formula E *equals* mc²". Smith went further by asserting that the title of Professor Einstein's Special Theory of Relativity, *Zür Elektro-*

---

[1] Moriarty told Holmes that he stood in the way "of a mighty organisation". *The Final Problem, S.,* p. 543.)

[2] *Ibid.,* p. 540.   [3] *Ibid.,* p. 540.   [4] *Ibid.,* p. 549.

[5] It was first published in *The Second Cab* (Boston, 1947) edited by James Keddie, Jr., and was reprinted in *Baker Street and Beyond, together with some Trifling Monographs* (Morristown, N.J., 1957), edited by Edgar W. Smith.

[6] As Holmes did his treatise on secret writings (*The Dancing Men, S.,* p. 630).

1

dynamik Bewegter Koerper ("On the Electrodynamics of Moving Bodies"), first published in *Ann. d. Physik*, June, 1905, was suggestively imitative of the title of Dr. Moriarty's *The Dynamics of an Asteroid*, which was certainly in print as early as 1888. On the other hand, Smith suggested that Moriarty's treatise may itself have been anticipated in some degree by Professor Charles Lutwidge Dodgson's *The Dynamics of a Particle*, published in 1865.

However this may be, Edgar Smith devoted an appreciable part of the remainder of his essay to taking to task those who had published fantastic theories about entirely speculative relationships between Moriarty and Holmes:

"Mr. T. S. Blakeney, for example, quotes an anonymous writer, who, basing his argument on the familiar fact that Moriarty and Holmes were never seen together by any third person, has made the frightening suggestion that Moriarty was Holmes himself.[1] Mr. Eustace Portugal, in somewhat similar vein, has made the cavalier assumption that it was Moriarty, and not the Great Detective himself, who returned from the Reichenbach—an assumption which calls for a very neat feat of impersonation indeed.[2] Mr. A. G. Macdonell, less drastic in his imaginings, has supposed that Holmes dragooned an obscure and innocent professor in one of the smaller English universities into lending his name to the feeding of a monstrous fiction built up by Holmes to bolster his fading reputation.[3] Father (now Monsignor) Ronald A. Knox, whose scholarship in the Canon frequently leaves a good deal more to be desired than the Higher Criticism he sought to satirize, has advanced the rather tentative and uninteresting thought that Mycroft Holmes was one of Moriarty's henchmen.[4] All of these theories, to borrow a technical phrase the master once employed, are 'unmitigated bleat'."[5]

This kind of writing is amusing and doubtless of interest, but it does not satisfy the student of biography. The omission is all

[1] T. S. Blakeney, *Sherlock Holmes: Fact or Fiction?* (London, 1932), Appendix III, pp. 130–4, "The Holmes–Moriarty Hypothesis".

[2] "The Holmes–Moriarty Duel", *The Bookman*, May, 1934.

[3] "The Truth about Professor Moriarty", *The New Statesman*, 5 October, 1929.

[4] "The Mystery of Mycroft" in *Baker Street Studies* (London, 1934) edited by H. W. Bell.

[5] Holmes's actual criticism of the contents of "the agony columns of the various London journals" was "Bleat, Watson—— unmitigated bleat!" (*The Red Circle*, *S.*, p. 952).

the more surprising when it is recalled that Moriarty was the predecessor, and in essentials the prototype, of both Mabuse and Fu-Manchu. Although it is true that in writing of the trial of the members of the Moriarty organisation Watson said that "of their terrible chief few details came out during the proceedings",[1] some facts are available to us in the literature. It is the additional purpose of this essay to demonstrate that other aspects of Moriarty's life can reasonably be deduced.

In our appreciation of the importance of Dr. Moriarty, we have to remember that Holmes said of him in 1891:

> "He is the organizer of half that is evil and of nearly all that is undetected in this great city. He is a genius, a philosopher, an abstract thinker. He has a brain of the first order. He sits motionless, like a spider in the centre of its web, but that web has a thousand radiations, and he knows well every quiver of each of them. He does little himself. He only plans. But his agents are numerous and splendidly organized."[2]

Three years earlier Holmes had described Dr. Moriarty to Watson in the following words, which are of considerable supplementary importance because they tell us what we know of the *magnum opus* of the scientific master-criminal:

> "The greatest schemer of all time, the organizer of every devilry, the controlling brain of the underworld—a brain which might have made or marred the destiny of nations. That's the man . . . the celebrated author of *The Dynamics of an Asteroid*—a book which ascends to such rarefied heights of pure mathematics that it is said that there was no man in the scientific press capable of criticizing it."[3]

In partial explanation of the title of this essay, which respectfully defies tradition, I would remark here that although virtually all references I have seen in the published Higher Criticism of the literature of Baker Street describe the arch-criminal as "Professor Moriarty",[4] this must clearly be regarded with tolerance as a mere courtesy title. It is true that "at the

---

[1] *The Final Problem, S.*, p. 556.   [2] *Ibid.*, p. 540.
[3] *The Valley of Fear, L.*, p. 460.
[4] See, for example, T. S. Blakeney, Lord Donegall, W. S. Baring-Gould, H. W. Bell, Vincent Starrett, Gavin Brend and E. B. Zeisler. Starrett on p. 33 of his classic *The Private Life of Sherlock Holmes* (London, 1934), writes of "Professor Robert Moriarty", but wisely omits this erroneous forename in the revised edition of 1961.

end of the 'eighties" in the Birlstone affair[1] Holmes quite correctly referred to Moriarty, "one of the first brains of Europe with all the powers of darkness at his back" as a Professor, and was able to quote his salary at that time from his unnamed university as £700 per annum, for the benefit of Inspector Alec MacDonald.[2] In April, 1891, however, at the beginning of the dramatic chain of events that culminated in the historic confrontation at the falls of Reichenbach, Holmes said of Moriarty to Watson:

> "His career has been an extraordinary one. He is a man of good birth and excellent education, endowed by Nature with a phenomenal mathematical faculty. At the age of twenty-one he wrote a treatise upon the Binomial Theorem, which has had a European vogue. On the strength of it, he won the Mathematical Chair at one of our smaller Universities, and had, to all appearance, a most brilliant career before him. But the man had hereditary tendencies of the most diabolical kind. A criminal strain ran in his blood, which, instead of being modified, was increased and rendered infinitely more dangerous by his extraordinary mental powers. Dark rumours gathered round him in the University town, and eventually he was compelled to resign his Chair and to come down to London, where he set up as an Army coach."[3]

This passage makes it clear that it was proper for Holmes to refer to the mathematical criminal as "ex-Professor Moriarty",[4] but suggests that it was less accurate for the great detective to describe him as "Mr. Moriarty" in Holmes's note to Watson written at the falls of Reichenbach.[5] To disagree with Holmes is distressing, but I find it almost impossible to believe that Moriarty's treatise upon the Binomial Theorem was not recognized by the award of a doctorate. I think it virtually certain, moreover, in view of what Holmes had said in 1888 of Moriarty's book, *The Dynamics of an Asteroid*, which was so

---

[1] *The Valley of Fear*, L., p. 467. For the proof that the action of the case started on 7 January, 1888, see Hall, (II), pp. 6–7.
[2] *Ibid.*, p. 472.   [3] *The Final Problem*, S., p. 539.   [4] *Ibid.*, p. 540.
[5] *Ibid.*, p. 555. It may be significant in this regard that when earlier in the same case Holmes addressed Moriarty directly as "Mr. Moriarty" (*ibid.*, p. 543) the master-criminal seems to have taken instant offence. The previous courtesies of the conversation were abruptly abandoned. Moriarty "snarled" that he would bring destruction upon Holmes, and forthwith turned his rounded back on the great detective and indignantly left the room.

brilliant in its conception and reached such rarefied heights in pure mathematics that nobody was capable of reviewing it, that this published work would have earned Moriarty an additional doctorate *honoris causa*.

If it is considered reasonable to believe that a man of Moriarty's towering intellect and outstanding scientific achievements would have obtained at least one doctorate as a matter of certainty, then in this respect the title of this essay is justified. There is, of course, absolute canonical authority for his Christian name from Holmes himself, who after the death of the master-criminal described him to Watson as "Professor James Moriarty, who had one of the great brains of the century".[1] It is true that Watson had made an earlier careless reference to Moriarty as the brother of Colonel James Moriarty,[2] but in my view no importance need be attached to this simple mistake. Watson even fell into the same error in regard to his own name, which he firmly stated to be "John H. Watson" in his very first account of a Holmes case in which he was involved,[3] afterwards inadvertently recording his first forename as "James" in the seventh of the published adventures in which he acted as Holmes's biographer.[4] One wonders, in parenthesis, if the name "James" had some special psychological significance for Watson, which caused him to flounder into a morass of uncertainty whenever he encounterd it.

One of the solid facts available to us is that Dr. Moriarty died on 4 May, 1891, at the falls of Reichenbach in Switzerland.[5] Holmes's first-hand account to Watson of the end of the brief struggle on that narrow ledge above the abyss, "that dreadful cauldron of swirling water and seething foam"[6] leaves us in no doubt on the point:

[1] *The Empty House*, S., p. 580.
[2] *The Final Problem*, S., p. 536. As Lt. Col. C. B. Appleby, the Director of the National Army Museum at Camberley, pointed out in a letter to *The Sunday Times* of 20 November, 1960, no Colonel James Moriarty appeared in the *Army List* during the relevant period of the nineteenth century.
[3] *A Study in Scarlet*, L., p. [3].
[4] *The Man with the Twisted Lip*, S., p. 125. I cannot resist recording, however, as a curious example of duplication of forenames, that in one of the lists of University Electors of Trinity College, Dublin, there are two different Rev. Thomas Moriarty's side by side. (*The Dublin University Calendar for the Year 1875*, Dublin, 1875, p. 552.)
[5] *The Final Problem*, S., p. 552 and *The Empty House*, S., p. 566.
[6] *The Final Problem*, S., p. 556.

"I slipped through his grip, and he with a horrible scream kicked madly for a few seconds and clawed the air with both his hands. But for all his efforts he could not get his balance, and over he went. With my face over the brink I saw him fall for a long way.[1] Then he struck a rock, bounded off, and splashed into the water."[2]

How old was Dr. Moriarty at his death? At first sight the evidence on the point is conflicting. We know from Inspector Alec MacDonald's description of him in 1888, for example, that Moriarty's hair at that time was already grey, and that his hand on the Inspector's shoulder "was like a father's blessing before you go out into the cold, cruel world".[3] Three years later in 1891, Holmes told Watson that at the conclusion of Moriarty's unheralded visit to Baker Street, "he turned his rounded back upon me and went peering and blinking out of the room".[4] Both these word-pictures give a clear impression of a man in his declining years.

On the other hand, in 1891 Moriarty was still physically active enough for Watson to describe him as "a tall man pushing his way furiously through the crowd" at Victoria Station,[5] and for the master-criminal deliberately to seek a final settlement with Holmes at the Reichenbach in unarmed combat. Since Holmes was only thirty-nine in 1891,[6] possessed of "iron strength"[7] and "undoubtedly one of the finest boxers of his weight" Watson had ever seen,[8] additionally skilled in "baritsu, or the Japanese system of wrestling",[9] it is clear that Moriarty must have known that in the encounter that he went to so much trouble to arrange, the great detective would be a most formidable antagonist. Yet Moriarty, "anxious to revenge himself" upon Holmes, "drew no weapon" but boldly rushed at his

---

[1] It is odd that Holmes did not follow precedent by making an impressive off-the-cuff calculation of the speed of Moriarty's descent, as he did of the train during a journey to Tavistock (*Silver Blaze, S.*, p. 306). A reasonable estimate of the height of the ledge above the rock, and the knowledge that the rate of acceleration of falling bodies is 32 feet per second per second, would have enabled him to be more enlightening about the force of the impact between Moriarty and the rock.

[2] *The Empty House, S.*, p. 566. [3] *The Valley of Fear, L.*, p. 471.
[4] *The Final Problem, S.*, p. 543. [5] *Ibid.*, p. 547.
[6] Holmes was born in 1852, according to the well-reasoned suggestion of his first biographer. (Blakeney, *op. cit.* p. 3.)
[7] *The Norwood Builder, S.*, p. 600. [8] *The Yellow Face, S.*, p. 334.
[9] *The Empty House, S.*, p. 566.

enemy and threw his long arms around him.[1] All this suggests in the most definite way that Moriarty, a man of superlative intelligence, believed that he had at least a reasonable chance of overcoming Holmes in this deliberately sought trial of physical strength and skill.[2]

The inference is therefore strong that Moriarty was by no means so old and decrepit as a hasty reading of some of the descriptions I have quoted might suggest. Probably he was not much older than Holmes himself. Moriarty's shoulders, as Holmes himself discerned, were "rounded from much study".[3] but may well have been immensely strong. The "peering and blinking", upon which Holmes remarked, was obviously one of those affectations common among eccentric academics irrespective of age. It is also fair to point out that when Alec MacDonald likened Moriarty to a father, the Inspector was a still "young but trusted member of the detective force", who was "far from having attained the national fame" that was later to be his. His bony figure only "gave promise" of his later exceptional strength.[4] Through the eyes of so young a man, age being relative, Moriarty could have seemed a father figure and yet have been under fifty.

With the evidence thus assembled from the canon, we are entitled to look again at a document, the veracity of which (in part) has been disputed by some.[5] I refer to the letter written by Dr. Moriarty's nephew, Mr. James Moriarty, to Dr. W. S. Bristowe, a leading member of the Sherlock Holmes Society of London, in 1960.[6] In this letter it is positively stated that Dr. Moriarty was born "about 1846", which would make him about 45 years old at the time of his death. It may be thought that this estimate of his age by a blood-relative coincides

[1] *The Empty House, S.*, p. 566.
[2] In this connexion it will be recalled that when the unarmed Moriarty, smiling and blinking, called unheralded at 221B Baker Street, "there was something about his eyes" that made even Holmes feel very glad that he had a loaded, cocked revolver on the table. (*The Final Problem, S..* p. 542.)
[3] *The Final Problem, S.*, p. 541.
[4] *The Valley of Fear, L.*, p. 467.
[5] In particular by the late Sir S. C. Roberts, who described it as "this final outburst of slanderous malice on the part of the Moriarty family", and by R. C. Mitchell, who wrote that he was "but one of many outraged by the cruel calumny to which you [*The Sunday Times*] gave space in your journal".
[6] *S.H.J.* Winter, 1960, pp. 6–14 and *The Sunday Times*, 13 November, 1960.

remarkably well with the other evidence we have considered. Since, moreover, the violent criticisms of the letter on the occasion of its publication in *The Sunday Times* were directed only at the attacks on the character of Holmes contained in it, it is not unreasonable for us to take some notice of the few simple facts about Moriarty revealed by his nephew which were not disputed by the critics, especially as most of these are confirmed by the canon. Mr. James Moriarty wrote, for example, that Dr. Moriarty "was never married", which we know to be true on the authority of Holmes,[1] and that his hobby was art, which to him "meant the purchase of pictures by Greuze and other artists costing thousands of pounds", which we also know to be true from the mute evidence in Moriarty's study observed by both Holmes and Inspector MacDonald.[2] In the same context we learn that Moriarty had at least six bank accounts, and that in 1888 he could afford to pay the chief of staff of his criminal organisation, Colonel Sebastian Moran, "the second most dangerous man in London",[3] a salary of no less than £6,000 a year.[4]

Holmes told Watson that Moriarty was "a man of good birth and excellent education".[5] We can be certain that he was of Irish descent (his name comes from the Irish *o'muiricerzaiz*) and it is difficult to set aside the evidence that connects him, as might properly be expected, with the distinguished family of Moriarty, which included David Moriarty (1814–1877), who became Bishop of Kerry in 1856.[6] David Moriarty was educated at Maynooth College, founded in 1795 for the training of students intended for the Irish priesthood. If the young James Moriarty followed the family tradition by starting his education at this fairly exclusive establishment, it seems entirely possible that some traces of this early ecclesiastical training and background still clung about him in his later life as a master-criminal, in precisely the same way that this "pale, and ascetic-looking" man retained "something of the professor in his looks" as late as 1891, according to Holmes.[7] In this connexion,

---

[1] *The Valley of Fear*, L., p. 473.　　　[2] *Ibid.*, p. 471.
[3] *The Empty House*, S., p. 580.　　　[4] *The Valley of Fear*, L., p. 474.
[5] *The Final Problem*, S., p. 539.
[6] *The Concise Dictionary of National Biography*, i, p. 904.
[7] *The Final Problem*, S., p. 541.

it seems to me to be of the greatest possible interest that Inspector Alec MacDonald said of Moriarty to Holmes and Watson:

"He'd have made a grand meenister, with his thin face and grey hair and solemn-like way of talking. When he put his hand on my shoulder as we were parting, it was like a father's blessing before you go out into the cold, cruel world."[1]

There is one assertion about Moriarty attributed to Holmes by Watson which is at complete variance with the great detective's statement that Moriarty was a man of good birth and excellent education, and with my own belief that he was a member of the well-known and distinguished Moriarty family. I refer, of course, to the astonishing remark by Holmes that Moriarty's brother was a station-master in the West of England.[2] Victorian station-masters were doubtless most excellent fellows, but they do not fit into the picture of the Church, the Army and Navy, academic and literary achievement and *Who's Who* conjured up by Holmes's firm and simple statement in *The Final Problem* that Dr. Moriarty was "a man of good birth and excellent education".

My belief is that Watson misheard Holmes in one small particular, which is readily demonstrated by reference to another distinguished member of the Moriarty family who was certainly alive in 1888, for he died in 1906. Captain Henry Augustus Moriarty, R.N., was awarded the C.B. for his navigation of the Great Eastern when laying the Atlantic cables, and gave evidence as a nautical expert before various parliamentary committees. He was the distinguished author of several authoritative technical volumes. He was a native of County Cork, and was the second son of Commander *James* [my italics] Moriarty, R.N. He was finally rewarded for his services to his country by his appointment as Queen's *harbour-master* [my italics] at Portsmouth.[3]

W. S. Baring-Gould, in his biography of Sherlock Holmes, gave a date of 1867 for the astonishing event recorded by

---

[1] *The Valley of Fear*, L., p. 471. [2] *Ibid.*, p. 473.
[3] *Concise DNB*, ii, p. 311.

Holmes, that at the age of twenty-one, Moriarty wrote his treatise on the Binomial Theorem, which was to have a European vogue.[1] I have been unable to discover the source from which the late Baring-Gould obtained the date of 1867, but it would be unreasonable to doubt it, since it coincides neatly with Mr. James Moriarty's statement that his uncle was born about 1846. This suggests that the young Moriarty obtained a place at his university at a fairly early age, probably in 1862, or 1863 at latest, which would not be impossible for a youthful genius. There can be no reasonable doubt, I fancy, that a member of the Moriarty family would enter an Irish university, and we can therefore say with confidence that it was the University of Dublin, Trinity College, which was founded in 1591, since neither the Queen's University of Belfast nor the National University of Ireland at Dublin existed until 1908. I have already shown, moreover, (p. 5, n. 4) that Trinity College, Dublin, was the *alma mater* of other members of the Moriarty family.

It is a great nuisance that the *Calendars* of Trinity College, which list the Scholars from the Restoration onwards, do not record the name of James Moriarty. I think it fair to point out, however, that these old works of reference were not always entirely accurate. I was able to show, for example, that Sherlock Holmes was unquestionably at Trinity College, Cambridge, on the solid basis of his remark to Watson that "Reginald Musgrave had been in the same college as myself".[2] I reproduced photographically the relevant page of the official list showing that "R. Musgrave" was an undergraduate at Trinity in 1870,[3] which left the matter in no doubt. It was, admittedly, curious that the publishers, Messrs. Deighton, Bell & Co. and Bell & Daldy, omitted Sherlock Holmes himself from the list. I was, however, able to demonstrate (again photographically) that the same firm of publishers had made an equally careless mistake in their production of a very successful book, *Hints for Pedestrians*, written by Watson's uncle, G. C. Watson, M.D.,

[1] *Sherlock Holmes. A Biography of the World's First Consulting Detective* (London, 1962), p. 20.
[2] *The Musgrave Ritual, S.*, p. 399.
[3] Hall, I, Plate ivb, and *The Cambridge University Calendar for the Year 1870* (Cambridge & London, 1870) p. 585.

which reached its third edition in 1863,[1] so that they were clearly not infallible.

Holmes told Watson, as we have seen, that on the strength of his treatise on the Binomial Theorem, Dr. Moriarty "won the Mathematical Chair at one of our smaller Universities",[2] but he failed to record which one. Fortunately for this inquiry (and for the country at the time) only a handful of universities existed in 1867 compared with the situation today. "Our smaller Universities" obviously excluded Oxford and Cambridge, and the University of London can clearly be left out of account, since when the dark rumours gathered round Dr. Moriarty in the University town, "he was compelled to resign his Chair and to come down to London, where he set up as an Army coach".[3]

I do not believe for one moment that Moriarty's Chair in Mathematics was at any of the four ancient Scottish universities that existed in 1867—those of St. Andrews, Glasgow, Edinburgh and Aberdeen. Had it been, I am convinced that Holmes would never have referred to it as "one of *our* [my italics] smaller Universities", for to him Scotland seems to have been as remote and alien as any foreign country. He was, almost militantly, the complete Englishman. It was in *England*, we recall, and not Great Britain, that for Holmes amateur sport was the best and soundest thing.[4] It was one of the most revered names in *England* that was being besmirched by a blackmailer, thus making it impossible for Holmes to leave London.[5] The cold and bitter east wind of the first war with Germany, Holmes warned Watson, would be "such a wind as never blew on *England* [my italics] yet".[6]

It is true that Aberdeen,[7] Dundee[8] and Edinburgh[9] are

---

[1] Hall, I, pp. 17 and 84, and Plates 1a and 1b.
[2] *The Final Problem*, S., p. 539.   [3] *Ibid.*, p. 539.
[4] *The Missing Three-Quarter*, S., p. 811.
[5] *The Hound of the Baskervilles*, L., p. 321.
[6] *His Last Bow*, S., p. 1086.
[7] Holmes remembered that cases not dissimilar to that of Lord St. Simon had occurred some years previously in Aberdeen and in Munich in the year after the Franco-Prussian war. (*The Noble Bachelor*, S., p. 237).
[8] The pips were set on the Openshaws in envelopes posted at Pondicherry in 1883, in Dundee in 1885 and in London in 1887. (*The Five Orange Pips*, S. pp. 107–12.)
[9] Mary Morstan told Holmes and Watson that from being "quite a child" to the age of seventeen, she had lived in "a comfortable boarding establishment at Edinburgh". (*The Sign of Four*, L., p. 153.)

mentioned casually in three of the sixty adventures, but they played no part of importance in the cases and Holmes showed no inclination to visit them. Indeed, if my reading of the canon is right, there is no record of Holmes having ever crossed the Border in his life. The only conceivable argument to the contrary would seem to rest on the flimsy foundation of Watson's infuriatingly vague reference, in a single phrase, to "the singular adventures of the Grice Patersons in the island of Uffa".[1] It is, I suppose, just possible that in the Western Isles there may be an uncharted island of this name, but I must place on record the fact that in none of my sailing and fishing holidays "among the farthest Hebrides"[2] have I ever heard of Uffa or the Grice Patersons.

Leaving Cambridge, Oxford and London out of account, as we have properly done, the three English universities existing in 1867 were Durham, Newcastle-upon-Tyne and Manchester. Which of these fits Holmes's two descriptive phrases "one of our smaller Universities" and "the University town", where the dark rumours gathered?[3] As to the first, Durham University was, and is, by far the smallest of the three and has the earliest foundation, 1832,[4] compared with Manchester (1851) and Newcastle (1852). As to the second phrase, which indicates that the town (or city) was to some extent dominated by and identified with the university, as in Oxford and Cambridge, this has never been true of Manchester and Newcastle. It was, however, entirely applicable to Durham, which at the 1901 census had a population of only 14,679, yet had an established educational tradition going back to the time of Prior Richard de Hoton (d. 1308) who erected a hall in Oxford for students from Durham, which later became Durham College, and later still Trinity College. Henry VIII had an unfulfilled intention of founding a college of his own at Durham.

For a man of Dr. Moriarty's ecclesiastical family connexions and early background, it must be obvious that the small University of Durham would have a considerable attraction.

---

[1] *The Five Orange Pips*, S., p. 103.
[2] William Wordsworth, "The Solitary Reaper", *Memorials of a Tour in Scotland*, 1803.
[3] *The Final Problem*, S., p. 539.
[4] Its doors were actually opened at Michaelmas, 1833.

Its first Warden, and a prime mover in its foundation, was Archdeacon Charles Thorp, whilst the governors included the dean and chapter of the cathedral. The visitor was the Bishop of Durham. The desirability of Durham for Moriarty would be increased by the fact that both the system and the life of the University were broadly similar to those of Oxford and Cambridge, as had been those of Moriarty's own University of Dublin, with its single, beautiful college of "the Holy and Undivided Trinity".

I think it probable that Moriarty, with his artistic appreciation of beauty proved by his fond possession of at least one priceless painting by Jean Baptiste Greuze,[1] spent some of his happiest years at Durham. Here, in close proximity to the great Cathedral, one of the most beautiful Norman buildings in England, towering above the River Wear, and to the magnificent partly Norman castle, he spent the best years of his young manhood as a successful Professor of Mathematics. There can be no doubt about his natural and persuasive ability and enthusiasm as a teacher. It will be remembered that Inspector Alec MacDonald told Holmes and Watson that he "had a chat with [Moriarty] on eclipses—how the talk got that way I canna think—but he had out a reflector lantern and a globe and made it all clear in a minute".[2] Here, too, in the peace and quietude of a university (in those days) he was able to enjoy the supreme, creative satisfaction of carrying out the research that enabled him to write his incomparable *The Dynamics of an Asteroid.*

As Holmes told Watson, Moriarty had "a most brilliant career before him. But the man had hereditary tendencies of the most diabolical kind. A criminal strain ran in his blood".[3] We know no details of the perversions and compulsions of Moriarty's Jekyll and Hyde existence during those last years at Durham, as he simultaneously built up his vast criminal organisation around his £6,000-a-year Chief of Staff in London, Colonel Sebastian Moran. They must have been pretty bad, I fancy, for Holmes to describe them as "diabolical", and for Watson to refer to them as "unutterable infamies".[4]

---

[1] *The Valley of Fear*, L., p. 471.   [2] *Ibid.*, L., p. 470.
[3] *The Final Problem*, S., p. 539.   [4] *Ibid.*, p. 549.

However that may be, we do know that some time after January, 1888[1] the dark rumours that had gathered round him at Durham compelled him to resign his Chair. One fancies that this must have been a considerable blow to Moriarty, who seems to have enjoyed the best of both worlds for some years as both a Professor and a master-criminal.

We know, at any rate, that he packed his bags, including his Greuze and his specially bound author's copy of *The Dynamics of an Asteroid*, and set up in London as an Army coach.[2] This was obviously a mere front for his principal activities, but we can be sure that it would be efficiently realistic. It may well have been suggested by Colonel Moran, whose military connexions would doubtless have enabled him to introduce the necessary nucleus of respectable pupils.

With the facts of Moriarty's life thus assembled, we can see that his period as a full-time criminal in London, engaged in the on-the-spot and day-to-day direction of his large organization, was in reality quite short. He was still a Professor in January, 1888, and he died in May, 1891, which limits this part of his life to about three years. When Holmes told Watson, therefore, that for "years past" he had been continuously conscious of "some deep organizing power which for ever stands in the way of the law", and a force of which he had felt the presence "again and again in cases of the most varying sorts—forgery cases, robberies, murders"[3], he was including those later years at Durham, from where Colonel Moran in London doubtless received by post a stream of directives and precisely planned schemes for crimes to be executed by the organization.[4] This assumption is supported by Holmes's remark, "He sits motionless . . . He does little himself. He only plans."[5] Obviously one could sit as motionless, and do as little, as efficiently in Durham as in London in Victorian times,

---

[1] He still had his Chair in that year (*The Valley of Fear*, L., p. 472).

[2] We may presume that he closed his Durham bank account, thus reducing the number of these to five.

[3] *The Final Problem*, S., pp. 539–40.

[4] This was perfectly practicable. In Fritz Lang's film-script *The Will of Dr. Mabuse* the master-criminal was incarcerated in a lunatic asylum, and Mabuse's directives were conveyed to his organisation by his psychiatrist.

[5] *The Final Problem*, S., p. 540.

particularly when the Post Office was a good deal more reliable than it is in our electronic age of apathy and incompetence.[1]

I hope that in this essay I have been able to add a few new touches to the portrait of the world's greatest genius of crime. A final point about Moriarty is that so far as I have been able to discover he enjoyed the distinction of being the one person for whose death Holmes was *directly* responsible and where we know this with *certainty*. As regards the first of these stipulations, the villain of Stoke Moran met his death from the poison fangs of his own swamp adder. Holmes remarked:

> "Some of the blows of my cane came home, and roused its snakish temper, so that it flew upon the first person it saw. In this way I am no doubt indirectly responsible for Dr. Grimesby Roylott's death, but I cannot say that it is likely to weigh very heavily upon my conscience."[2]

The death of Tonga, the Andaman islander, during the pursuit of the *Aurora* near Plumstead Marshes on the Thames, comes into the second category of *uncertainty*, for we simply do not know whether Holmes or Watson fired the fatal bullet that saved them from a poisoned dart from Tonga's blow-pipe:

> "Even as we looked he plucked out from under his covering a short, round piece of wood, like a school-ruler, and clapped it to his lips. Our pistols rang out together. He whirled round, threw up his arms, and, with a kind of choking cough, fell sideways into the stream. I caught one glimpse of his venomous, menacing eyes amid the white swirl of the waters."[3]

One thing is certain. Holmes had no regrets in regard to the death of Moriarty. Before Reichenbach, he said to Watson:

> "Your memoirs will draw to an end, Watson, upon the day that I crown my career by the capture or *extinction* [my italics] of the most dangerous and capable criminal in Europe."[4]

At Reichenbach, Holmes wrote in his note to his old friend:

> "I have already explained to you, however, that my career had in any case reached its crisis, and that no possible conclusion to it could be more congenial to me than this."[5]

---

[1] As an example of one's experience today, the Post Office is unable to tell me who signed for a vanished parcel containing a £12 book sent by Recorded Delivery to the office of *The Book Collector* in London.
[2] *The Speckled Band, S.*, pp. 200–1.   [3] *The Sign of Four, L.*, p. 235.
[4] *The Final Problem, S.*, p. 551.   [5] *Ibid.*, pp. 555–6.

II

SHERLOCK HOLMES
AND SIGMUND FREUD
A Study in Forgery

*T*HE *Seven-Per-Cent Solution. Being a Reprint from the Reminiscences of John H. Watson, M.D., as edited by Nicholas Meyer*, was published in 1975. In his Foreword Mr. Meyer quotes a letter written to him by his uncle Henry in 1970, in which the latter claimed to have discovered in the attic of his house in Hampshire an unpublished book-length typescript dictated by Dr. Watson during his last years in an old people's home, which he had entered in 1932. In what he called the "Introductory" section of the typescript, which Mr. Meyer subsequently and invariably describes as a manuscript, the signatory, claiming to be "John H. Watson, M.D.", said that it was prepared in 1939, when he was eighty-seven years old.

Mr. Meyer concedes in the first paragraph of his Foreword that the discovery of an unpublished manuscript about Sherlock Holmes by Dr. Watson, a more improbable event in the nature of things than the unearthing of a further Dead Sea Scroll, may well be regarded with scepticism in the world of letters. He tells us, however, that he believes it to be genuine, and he has produced from it a very successful book, thus making this remarkable tale available to a wide audience. I must say now on behalf of the faithful fundamentalists, the devotees of the true and original Baker Street canon that is so cruelly violated by

16

this alleged discovery, that we cannot fail to regard it with the gravest suspicion. Can we really believe that Moriarty was not a criminal at all, and that the whole of Holmes's classic struggle with "the Napoleon of crime",[1] recorded for us by the true Dr. Watson in *The Final Problem* and *The Valley of Fear*, never occurred at all? Are we seriously expected to accept, as the dubious Dr. Watson of the new MS. tells us, that Moriarty was a little,[2] whining[3] man, an innocent and impecunious mathematics teacher at Roylott School, "one of the lesser known public schools in the area of West London",[4] who never wrote a treatise on the Binomial Theorem,[5] and yet very oddly introduced himself to the pseudo-Watson by means of a visiting card bearing the name "Professor Moriarty"?[6]

If young Mr. Meyer's uncle Henry boasted a surname, and an address less imprecise than merely "London",[7] there are a number of simple, preliminary questions one would like to address to this gentleman. What, for example, of Colonel Sebastian Moran, "the second most dangerous man in London",[8] Moriarty's chief of staff,[9] who was paid a salary of no less than £6,000 a year in 1887?[10] He at least can scarcely have been a figment of the imagination of the genuine and beloved Dr. Watson, or a cocaine-induced dream experienced by Holmes, since Colonel Moran was arrested by Inspector Lestrade, an independent and impeccable witness.[11] What of Moriarty's taste for £4,000 paintings by Jean Baptiste Greuze, an example of which was seen and vouched for by another official witness, Inspector Alec MacDonald?[12] How can we reconcile such sums of money and art treasures, and a known association with a notorious criminal like Colonel Moran, with a Moriarty who was an inoffensive mathematics teacher and nothing else?

In the hoo-ha of a supposedly new and dramatic literary discovery of this kind, it is a trifle wearisome to have to read yet again the fable of how in 1862 Moriarty became the private tutor of the youthful Sherlock Holmes.[13] This unlikely tale was

---

[1] *The Final Problem*, S., p. 540.
[2] Meyer, p. 37.
[3] Meyer, pp. 37–8.
[4] Meyer, p. 37.
[5] Meyer, p. 38.
[6] Meyer, p. 34.
[7] Meyer, pp. 9–11.
[8] *The Empty House*, S., p. 580.
[9] *The Valley of Fear*, L., p. 474.
[10] *Ibid.*, L., p. 474.
[11] *The Empty House*, S., p. 576.
[12] *The Valley of Fear*, L., p. 471.
[13] Meyer, p. 39.

first put about over a dozen years ago by the late W. S. Baring-Gould,[1] and was therefore readily available in print to the putative forger, Mr. Meyer's "uncle Henry", who did not write to his credulous nephew until March, 1970, enclosing the MS. together with the dubious story of its discovery. The suggestion by Baring-Gould that the great detective and Moriarty had known each other since Holmes was a boy was demolished by me in print in 1969[2] on the evidence of the text of *The Final Problem*, which demonstrates that Holmes's description of the encounter between Moriarty and himself in 1891 was their first meeting face-to-face:

> "He peered at me with great curiosity in his puckered eyes. 'You have less frontal development than I should have expected', he said at last."[3]

It is a nuisance to have to repeat a correction of this error, arising from the forger's lack of acquaintance with the relevant literature, but the opportunity can at least be taken of nailing the mistake to the wall forever (one hopes) by additionally reminding the over-credulous Mr. Meyer of an exchange between Inspector Alec Macdonald and Holmes in the historic sitting-room in Baker Street "at the end of the 'eighties":[4]

> " 'I thought you told me once, Mr. Holmes, that you have never met Professor Moriarty?'
> 'No, I never have.' "[5]

The manuscript is mainly, but not wholly, composed of a mixture of a distorted text of *The Final Problem*, and the whole of the research on which an essay, "The Early Years of Sherlock Holmes", published by me in 1969,[6] was based. Mr. Meyer recognised the provenance of the latter for what it was, despite his swallowing of his uncle's unlikely tale, as he himself confesses on pages 215 and 223 of his edited version of the pseudo-Watson's MS., coupled with compliments to myself. Built on to this plagiarism, however, is a curious story of a visit by Holmes and Watson to Vienna in the Spring of 1891, a cruel violation of the classical true account of the "Great Hiatus"

[1] *op. cit.*, p. 20
[2] Hall, I, p. 41.
[3] *The Final Problem, S.*, p. 541.
[4] *The Valley of Fear, L.*, p. 467.
[5] *Ibid., L.*, p. 472.
[6] Hall, I, pp. 18–35.

between *The Final Problem* (1891) and *The Empty House* (1894) in Holmes's career as a consulting detective. This journey was allegedly made so that Holmes could be cured by Dr. Sigmund Freud of his addiction to cocaine, an addiction dating back to the detective's years as an undergraduate at Trinity College, Cambridge where, as I observed eight years ago in print, Holmes moped in his rooms with "no points of contact at all' with the other undergraduates,[1] and ultimately "loathed every form of society".[2] This trauma, as I explained, was undoubtedly caused by a tragedy involving both his parents which caused Holmes's "early addiction to cocaine, unquestionably used by him in the first years after his parents' deaths to dispel the spectre that haunted him".[3] Holmes's brother Mycroft was naturally similarly affected, and became "one of the queerest men" in London and was seen nowhere else but at his lodgings in Pall Mall, his office in Whitehall or the Diogenes Club. Mycroft was one of the founders of this extraordinary refuge for "the most unsociable and unclubbable men in town", where "no member is permitted to take the least notice of any other one".[4] Holmes's "aversion to women"[5] was thus explained, by his mother's "dreadful record of sin"[6] that had besmirched the household of his young days and caused his "father to take the law into his owns hands and obliterate by their deaths the 'hidden wickedness' (*The Copper Beeches, S.,* p. 286) of Mrs. Holmes and her paramour".[7]

Why the pseudo-Watson of the MS. considered it necessary for the tragic story of his mother's death and his father's suicide to be dredged from Holmes's unconscious mind under hypnosis by Freud I do not know. I was able to work out the whole simple cause and effect by a normal study of the ample clues provided by the literature of Baker Street, as Mr. Meyer concedes in a footnote on page 215 of his book. "This amazing event was actually deduced by Trevor Hall in his essay, 'The Early Years of Sherlock Holmes' . . ." I also tried to show in my book that this early tragedy undoubtedly influenced Holmes's choice of a career:

[1] *The "Gloria Scott", S.,* p. 375.
[2] *A Scandal in Bohemia, S.,* p. 3.
[3] Hall, I, p. 33.
[4] *The Greek Interpreter, S.,* pp. 479–80.
[5] *Ibid.,* p. 478.
[6] *The Copper Beeches, S.,* p. 286.
[7] Hall, I, p. 34.

19

"More importantly, Holmes was assuming the role of his own psychiatrist. Instead of allowing the traumatic experience to sink into his subconscious mind to fester, he was determined to bring it into the open and overcome it. The air of London (and of course the air of Sussex, Surrey and the other counties in which so many of his cases were located) was to be made sweeter, as he expressed it in retrospect to Watson, by his dedication to the exposure and punishment of 'hidden wickedness'. Whether the psychological healing was completely successful is a matter upon which opinion may be divided. Holmes's life gradually became purposeful and content, and he was able to overcome in time his early addiction to cocaine, which he unquestionably used in the first years after his parents' deaths to dispel the spectre that haunted him. He ultimately found it possible to return to East Sussex. On the other hand, Watson never recorded that Holmes finally overcame the manic-depression, the rhythmic alternation 'from extreme languor to devouring energy', and from good spirits to black melancholia, which the cruel blow he suffered in his early twenties undoubtedly caused."[1]

It will be seen that I wrote eight years ago that Holmes almost certainly cured himself, consciously and bravely, of both his cocaine addiction and its underlying cause, which was a painful memory of his most impressionable years. As I am sure that this view is shared by my fellow-fundamentalists and devoted admirers of the best and wisest man Watson had ever known, oblivion would seem to be the appropriate resting-place for the story that Holmes, suffering from drug-induced delusions that a simple teacher of mathematics was a master-criminal, became a patient of Sigmund Freud. Since, however, the scenes and conversations in Vienna constitute the only serious part of the MS. allegedly found by Mr. Meyer's uncle in his attic that is not easily recognizable as having been extracted from published sources, these pages are of interest to the textual critic. It is possible that from them we may learn something of the intellectual stature of the forger, and of the accuracy of the research he employed in his examination of the circumstances of Sigmund Freud in 1891, the year of his alleged meeting with Sherlock Holmes.

The dating of the journey from London and the action in

[1] Hall, i, p. 33.

Vienna covered by the MS. seems roughly to coincide with that of *The Final Problem*, that is to say from 24 April, 1891, to 4 May of the same year. These dates, which mark the period of ten days between Holmes, confessedly afraid of airguns, walking into Watson's consulting-room "looking even paler and thinner than usual", and the final encounter with Moriarty at the Reichenbach, are firmly recorded in the canon[1] and accepted by H. W. Bell.[2] The journey of Holmes and Watson on the continent of Europe is well-documented, including their crossing from Newhaven to Dieppe,[3] their first stay of two days in Brussels, "moving on upon the third day as far as Strasbourg", where Holmes received the telegram from London informing him that although the gang had been arrested, Moriarty had escaped. He received this disturbing news, it will be recalled, "with a bitter curse".[4] The remainder of the ten days was taken up by a continuance of the journey to Geneva, followed by "a charming week" during which the two friends "wandered up the valley of the Rhone" and made their way via the Gemmi Pass and Interlaken to Meiringen,[5] which was reached on 3 May, 1891.[6] Despite the dramatic outcome on the following day, it was clearly a leisurely affair.

The alternative tale told in the MS. at least followed the true account by starting with the scene in Watson's consulting-room, and Holmes's fear of airguns, on 24 April, 1891.[7] The duplicated journey to Geneva was a much more business-like and rapid example of foreign travel, however, with no diversions such as two days of sight-seeing in Brussels. In this version Holmes and Watson went to Paris, via Dover and Calais, and at the Gare du Nord caught the Vienna express, described by the pseudo-Holmes as fast and efficient. "The train we are taking makes only these stops that all the Continental expresses make",[8] he observed. It is reasonable to assume from this that the forger of the MS. intended to give the impression that Geneva would be reached more quickly than in the standard version of the story. From Geneva the Vienna express went

[1] *The Final Problem*, S., pp. 537–8 and 552.
[2] H. W. Bell, *Sherlock Holmes and Dr. Watson. The Chronology of their Adventures* (London, 1932), p. 72.
[3] *The Final Problem*, S., p. 549. [4] *Ibid.*, p. 550. [5] *Ibid.*, p. 550.
[6] *Ibid.*, p. 552. [7] Meyer, p. 21. [8] Meyer, p. 81.

straight on, we are told, via Berne, Zürich, Munich, Salzburg[1] and Linz[2] to Vienna. During the entire journey from Paris to Vienna the two friends only twice slept and "went through the process of shaving and donning clean linen",[3] which provides us with fairly solid evidence on which to base an estimate of at least the approximate date of the arrival of Holmes and Watson at Sigmund Freud's house in Vienna.[4]

If I read the forgery aright, which in places is not the simplest of tasks, we are told that the two friends spent the nights of 24 and 25 April in London, with possibly one night in Calais,[5] followed by two further nights aboard the Vienna express. This suggests that they would be in the Austrian capital before the end of April, 1891, but the date is not critical in our assessment of the credibility of the forgery. Indeed, only in the event of Holmes and Watson having remained on the Vienna express for a continuous period extending from April to August, 1891, is the forger's story saved from being reduced to nonsense, as we shall see.

The MS. found by "Uncle Henry" leaves us in no doubt in regard to the address in Vienna to which the two friends made their way immediately on their arrival in the capital:

> "Here one found the fashionable and oldest quarter of the town with the Graben, its busy street of shops and cafes, to the north of which, at Bergasse [*sic*] 19, dwelt Dr. Freud".[6]

The misspelling of Berggasse throughout the entire MS. is very odd, demonstrating, we may think, the forger's lack of acquaintance with Vienna. Meaning, as of course Berggasse does, "mountain street", it is even more curious to find the forger referring to it in at least one instance as "Bergasse street".[7] These oddities, however, pale into insignificance when we recall that Freud did not live there until August, 1891, as his biographer makes plain in his account of the family's first home following the marriage, and their move from it five years later:

> "There were four large rooms in the flat. The address was 8 Maria Theresienstrasse, their entrance to the block being there,

[1] Meyer, p. 83. [2] Meyer, p. 85.
[3] Meyer, pp. 82 and 86. [4] Meyer, p. 90.
[5] Meyer, p. 81. The forger's text is imprecise on the point.
[6] Meyer, p. 109. [7] Meyer, p. 112.

on the side opposite to the Schottenring. The Freuds' eldest child, Mathilde, was the first to be born in the new building, on October 16, 1887 . . . Three children, a daughter and two sons (October, 16, 1887; December 6, 1889; and February 19, 1891), were born in the first domicile. The sons were named Jean Martin after Charcot (not after Luther, as has been said) and Oliver after Cromwell, Freud's early hero. More room was needed for the growing family, so in August, 1891, they removed to the well-known address of 19 Berggasse which had the added advantage of being less expensive."[1]

Later in the first volume of the biography we learn more of 19 Berggasse:

"The roomier flat in the Berggasse, to which the Freuds had moved in the late summer of 1891, was not proving equal to the increasing number of children, so Freud rented another flat in 1892. This was on the ground floor in the same house, and gave on to a small but pleasant garden in the back. It had three rooms, used as patients' waiting-room, consulting-room and study respectively, so that Freud had every opportunity for quiet concentration. This arrangement lasted until 1907."[2]

With the facts of the matter before us, it is of further interest to read the forger's fanciful description of the interior of 19 Berggasse, as entered from the street, put into the mouth of the pseudo-Watson:

"We nodded and followed [the maid] inside, finding ourselves in a small but elegant entrance hall with a white marble floor. The house was some kind of Viennese chocolate bread miniature, crammed with Dresden knick-knacks of every description. To one side, a thin black banistered staircase led up to a charming little balcony that ran in a semi-circle over our heads."[3]

Since we know that Freud did not occupy the ground floor of 19 Berggasse until 1892, the MS. cannot be anything but a forgery, it would seem, unless we are invited to believe that Holmes and Watson spent a period of at least eight months aboard the Vienna express.

At his first meeting with Freud, the pseudo-Holmes tried to

[1] Ernest Jones, *Sigmund Freud: Life and Work* (3 vols., London, 1953, 1955 and 1957), i, pp. 164 and 167.
[2] *Ibid.*, p. 361.   [3] Meyer, p. 90.

emulate one of the favourite feats of the world's greatest detective. It was in the tradition exemplified in August, 1895, when "a wild-eyed and frantic young man, pale, dishevelled and palpitating", burst into the familiar room in Baker Street, announcing himself as "the unhappy John Hector McFarlane". Holmes remarked:

> "You mentioned your name as if I should recognize it, but I assure you that beyond the obvious facts that you are a solicitor, a Freemason, and an asthmatic, I know nothing whatever about you."

The young man "stared in amazement".[1] Following this pattern, the Holmes of the forged MS. told Freud that he "was born in Hungary", at which astonishing disclosure, "Freud stared at Holmes for a moment in utter shock".[2] This reaction was scarcely surprising, we may think, since "Sigmund Freud was born at 6.30 p.m. on the sixth of May, 1856, at 117 Schlossergasse, Freiberg, in Moravia".[3] The real Holmes was not entirely infallible, as is demonstrated by his frank observation to Watson in the matter of Mr. Neville St. Clair:

> "I think, Watson, that you are now standing in the presence of one of the most absolute fools in Europe. I deserve to be kicked from here to Charing Cross."[4]

In the matter of Freud's birthplace, however, the mistake of the pseudo-Holmes may be thought to be remarkable, since when he explained his methods to Freud he remarked that "your Balkanised accent hints at Hungary or Moravia".[5] However, our experience of the pseudo-Holmes suggests that if it was possible to get anything wrong, even with only two alternatives available, he could be relied upon to do so.

On page 121 of the MS. the pseudo-Watson wrote:

> Dr. Freud's discussion of other patients appeared to hold no interest for [Holmes] whatever, and I am afraid I was so preoccupied with Holmes's slightest reactions that I scarcely heard

---

[1] *The Norwood Builder*, S., p. 585. [2] Meyer, pp. 94–5.
[3] Jones, *op. cit.*, p. 1 and James Strachey, "Sigmund Freud. A Sketch of his Life and Ideas" in *The Psychopathology of Everyday Life. Sigmund Freud. Edited by James Strachey and translated from the German by Alan Tyson* (London, 1975), p. 11.
[4] *The Man with the Twisted Lip*, S., p. 143. [5] Meyer, p. 98.

anything of the Doctor's cases either. I have a dim recollection that he referred to them by the strangest names, sometimes alluding to the 'Rat Man' or the 'Wolf Man', and sometimes to a person called 'Anna O'. I understood him to be protecting the true identities of these people for reasons of professional discretion . . . Often, falling asleep with my thoughts idly touching on this and that, I have recalled those snatches of table talk in the Freud home and smiled to think of the man who looked like a rat and the one who resembled a wolf. And what of Anna O? Was her person perhaps sensationally rotund?"

We can leave Anna O. out of account, since she was the patient, not of Freud, but of Dr. Josef Breuer (1842–1925). Anna was one of the classical cases of hysteria, and far from being rotund, was an extremely attractive young woman, who "inflamed the heart of the psychiatrist in charge" of the sanatorium.[1] As regards the cases of the "Rat-Man" and the "Wolf-Man", however, we must presume that the forger decided that the MS. would be more saleable to a publisher in today's climate if an ingredient of occultism was included in it. Freud, therefore, was presented by the forger with the talents of foreknowledge and prevision in 1891 (or 1892) since the two patients respectively referred to under these curious labels did not come under his care until October, 1907[2] and February, 1908.[3] Pages 321 and 27 of *The Psychopathology of Everyday Life* tell us, moreover, that the case-history of the "Rat-Man" was not written until 1909, and that the "Wolf-Man" (Freud's "last major case history") was not written until 1914, and was not published until 1918.

We are told in the pseudo-Watson's MS. that in order to assist Holmes's treatment for his cocaine-addiction, by means of occupational therapy, Freud had "wired to England" in 1891 for the great detective's precious Stradivarius violin. When the parcel arrived, it was unpacked by Freud's daughter Anna, after her father had cut the string.[4] The pseudo-Watson tells us that Anna was "a girl of about five",[5] which we may think was a very youthful age for her to have been entrusted

---

[1] Jones, *op. cit.*, pp. 245–8. Anna O's entry in the index is "See Breuer".
[2] Jones, *op. cit.*, ii, p. 294.
[3] Jones, *op. cit.*, ii, p. 308.
[4] Meyer, p. 128.
[5] Meyer, p. 113.

with a task of this importance, assuming that there is any truth in the story whatsoever, which there is not. Anna, Freud's youngest daughter, was not born until the end of 1895.

From Freud's biographer we learn (as has already been quoted in another context) that the Freuds' first child, Mathilde, was born at 8 Maria Theresienstrasse on 16 October, 1887.[1] At the same address Jean Martin and Oliver were born on 6 December, 1889, and 19 February, 1891.[2] On page 245 of the biography we learn:

> "Freud's eldest daughter was named after Breuer's[3] wife [Mathilde Breuer] and his youngest after a sister of Breuer's son-in-law—incidentally a favourite patient of Freud's [Anna Hammerschlag, the daughter of Freud's old schoolteacher]."

Anna was the second of the two younger daughters who with Ernst, the third son (making up the family of six) were born at 19 Berggasse, her date of birth being 3 December, 1895, over four years after the forger's pretty story of her unpacking of Holmes's Stradivarius.[4] We begin to wonder whether this gentleman was capable of getting anything right at all. A glance at the "Chronological Table" of the principal events in Freud's life on pages 25–8 of *The Psychopathology of Everyday Life*, already quoted, which was available in English in 1960, first published by the Hogarth Press and the Institute of Psycho-Analysis, would have told him in the convenience of one place that Freud's six children and their years of birth were Mathilde, 1887; Jean Martin, 1889; Oliver, 1891; Ernst, 1892; Sophie, 1893; Anna, 1895.[5]

On pages 151–4 of the forgery we are told how Holmes and Watson accompanied Freud to the "fabled Vienna Opera House", where they were introduced to "Hugo Von [*sic*] Hofmannsthal", declared by the forger to be a "grave, middle-aged man", who described it as an honour to meet "Herr

---

[1] Jones, *op. cit.*, p. 164.   [2] Jones, *op. cit.*, p. 167·
[3] Dr. Joseph Breuer was Freud's close friend and associate.
[4] Jones, *op. cit.*, p. 167.
[5] Like Holmes, quoted a page or so previously, I too "deserve to be kicked from here to Charing Cross" for stupidity. While I was searching biographies of Freud for Anna's date of birth, *Who's Who* 1973, was within reach on my bookshelf. Anna Freud's entry on p. 1149 confirms her birth on 3 December, 1895.

Sherlock Holmes and Dr. John Watson". Not to be outdone in these courtesies, Holmes replied that it was no less an honour for Watson and himself to meet the author of *Gestern*, a work of which the pseudo-Watson confessed in the MS. that he had never heard. While Watson was brooding on his lack of knowledge, Holmes "engaged Von [*sic*] Hofmannsthal in an animated discussion of his operas, and quizzed him about his collaborator, someone named Richard Strauss". I find myself much in sympathy with Watson's puzzlement in regard to these matters, which it may be instructive to examine.

Hugo von Hofmannsthal (1874–1929) the "grave, middle-aged man"[1] of the MS., was seventeen years old in 1891. His first work, *Gestern, Studie in einen Akt, in Reimen*,[2] was a pamphlet of 46 pages privately printed in Vienna in 1891, under the pseudonym of Loris Theophil Morren.[3] We may therefore sympathise with Watson, who had never heard of it, and wonder a little at Holmes's supposed familiarity with this obscure, pseudonymous, privately printed little work. We may do more than wonder, moreover, at Holmes's "animated discussion" of Hofmannsthal's operas and his collaboration with Richard Strauss[4] in 1891. When we glance at the standard works of reference, which one would have thought were readily available to the forger, we see that there is not a word of truth in any of this tale.

Loewenberg tells us that *Elektra* was the first libretto written by Hofmannsthal (after Sophocles) for Richard Strauss, and that it was first performed in 1909.[5] This is amplified by Blom:

> "The first performance of 'Elektra', set to the first libretto written for Strauss by Hugo von Hofmannsthal, was at Dresden on 25 January, 1909 and the composer conducted it in London in March, 1910, after its first performance here by Beecham."[6]

[1] Meyer, p. 154.
[2] *Yesterday, Study in one Act, in Rhyme.*
[3] Gero von Wilport and Adolf Gühring, *Erstansgaben Deutscher Ditchtung, Eine Bibliographie zür Deutschen Literatur* (Stuttgart, 1967), p. 576. (*First Editions of German Books, A Bibliography of German Literature.*)
[4] Meyer, p. 154.
[5] Alfred Loewenberg, *Annals of Opera, 1597–1940. Compiled from the Original Sources* (Cambridge, 1943), p. 673.
[6] *Grove's Dictionary of Music and Musicians. Edited by Eric Blom* (Fifth Edition, London, 1954), vol. viii, p. 125.

In their bibliography of German first editions, Wilport and Gühring record for us:

"Hofmannsthal, H. von. *Elektra. Tragödie in einen Aufzug Frei nach Sophokles* (Berlin, 1904)."[1]

According to the forger, therefore, Holmes was discussing Hofmannsthal's "operas" in collaboration with Richard Strauss *thirteen years* before the first example was written and published, and *eighteen years* before its first performance.

There is no need, perhaps to prolong the agony, except to point to the fundamental error of the forger, who seems to have imagined that in April, 1891, Freud, not yet 35 years old, was a psycho-analyst of world-wide fame. Unfortunately the supposed "psychiatric department"[2] (or "Psychiatric Wing")[3] of the "great teaching hospital of Vienna, to which he had been [supposedly] formerly attached",[4] did not exist in 1891. Freud had worked for fourteen months in Franz Scholz's *Nervenabteilung*, but had subsequently been transferred first to the Department of Ophthalmology and then to the Department of Dermatology, in the normal course of his general training in medicine.[5] He studied under Charcot at the Salpêtrière (hospital for nervous diseases) in Paris.

James Strachey tells us that the revealing correspondence between Freud and his friend Wilhelm Fliess, a Berlin ear and throat specialist, over many years, shows that the former sent the latter his 40,000-word essay "Project for a Scientific Psychology". It was composed in 1895, the year Strachey calls "the water-shed of Freud's career" when he was moving from physiology to psychology.[6] He used the word "psycho-analysis" for the first time in 1896.[7] Strachey adds that it was only "after some ten years, in about 1906", that Freud attracted the adhesion of a number of Swiss psychiatrists to his views, to be followed by lectures in Salzburg in 1908 and in the United States in 1909.[8]

In 1891, however, these achievements were all in the future. It was in this year, indeed, still as a neurologist, that Freud

---

[1] Wilport and Gühring, *ibid.*, p. 576.   [2] Meyer, pp. 109–10.
[3] Meyer, p. 133.   [4] Meyer, p. 109.   [5] Jones, *op. cit.*, pp. 79–80.
[6] *The Psychopathology of Everyday Life*, pp. 15–16.
[7] *Ibid.*, p. 26.   [8] *Ibid.*, p. 16.

published his first book, *Aphasia*, dealing with the inability to express thought in words by reason of brain disease. It did not meet with the success it no doubt deserved. Of the 850 copies printed only 257 were sold over a period of nine years, when the rest were pulped. Freud received the equivalent of a few pounds in royalties (156.60 gulden).[1] His name did not appear in the index of the eleventh edition of the *Encyclopaedia Britannica* (Cambridge, 1910–11).

Faithful Sherlockians can, I fancy, forget the intrusion of *The Seven-Per-Cent Solution* into their peaceful lives. They can return with relief to the familiar pages of *The Final Problem*, confidently retaining their faith in the true story of what happened to Holmes, Watson and Moriarty in 1891.

[1] Jones, *op. cit.*, p. 237. Freud's biographer, writing in 1953, declared that there is no copy of *Aphasia* in any library in Great Britain.

III

THE CHEMICAL CORNER

by the Venerable Charles O. Ellison

THREE verdicts were passed at different times on Sherlock Holmes's knowledge of chemistry: one by young Stamford, who originally brought Holmes and Watson together, and two by Watson himself. Stamford spoke of Holmes as a "first-class chemist",[1] and Watson described his knowledge of chemistry first as "profound",[2] and later, more accurately, when he was better acquainted with his room-mate, as "eccentric".[3] The purpose of this chapter is to look at Holmes's chemical equipment and work in order to see what real part, if any, they played in his practice as a consultant detective.

The Baker Street "chemical corner" is first so described by Watson when he re-visits No. 221B following his dramatic re-union with Holmes in 1894. He observes "Our old chambers had been left unchanged, through the supervision of Mycroft Holmes and the immediate care of Mrs. Hudson. As I entered I saw, it is true, an unwonted tidiness, but the old landmarks were all in their places. There were the chemical corner and the acid stained deal-topped table . . ."[4] But domestic chemical activities had been carried on even in the Montague Street days. Referring to this period, Holmes remarks "All this occurred during the first months of the long vacation. I went up to my

---

[1] *A Study in Scarlet*, L., p. 8.   [2] *Ibid.*, p. 18.
[3] *The Five Orange Pips*, S., p. 116.
[4] *The Empty House*, S., p. 578. (cf. *The Mazarin Stone*, S., p. 1140, where "the acid-charred bench of chemicals" was still in place).

London rooms, where I spent seven weeks working out a few experiments in organic chemistry."[1] It seems unlikely that such experiments would have been permitted in his rooms when Holmes was *in statu pupillari* at the University. But the chemical equipment was removed to Baker Street where it formed part of the familiar scene along with the coal-scuttle, the violin, the gasogene, the works of reference, and all the other "landmarks" —as Watson terms them.

In addition to the acid stained table, other items of chemical significance are mentioned in the course of the stories. These include retorts, distillation apparatus,[2] "a formidable array of bottles and test-tubes",[3] "a bunsen burner", a condenser and "a two-litre measure", a "glass pipette" and "litmus-paper".[4] Nowhere is there any mention of a cold water supply, or a sink, without which practical chemical work would be at least severely handicapped. For instance, we are told of an occasion when "Holmes was seated at his side-table in his dressing-gown and working hard over a chemical investigation. A large curved retort was boiling furiously in the bluish flame of a Bunsen burner, and the distilled drops were condensing into a two-litre measure."[5] The process of distillation and condensation could not possibly be carried on, at any rate on a domestic scale, without a supply of running cold water to keep the condenser cool, and a sink to drain the water away. It is highly unlikely that these facilities were ever available in a Victorian sitting-room, and there is not a shred of evidence to suggest that the room in Baker Street was any exception in this respect.

There are numerous references throughout the saga to "maladorous experiments" which, on one occasion, were sufficiently obnoxious to render the room uninhabitable. To quote Watson. "[Holmes] busied himself all the evening in an abstruse chemical analysis which involved much heating of retorts and distilling of vapours, ending at last in a smell which fairly drove me out of the apartment".[6] In parenthesis, one wonders if Watson would have been justified in claiming a reduction in his share of the rent. Mrs. Hudson, too, might well

[1] The "Gloria Scott", S., p. 380. [2] The Sign of Four, L., p. 219.
[3] A Case of Identity, S., p. 69. [4] The Naval Treaty, S., p. 500.
[5] Ibid., p. 500. [6] The Sign of Four, L., p. 219.

have complained. Not for nothing is she described as "a long-suffering woman", and "weird and often malodorous scientific experiments" are included among her many trials.[1] She and Dr. Watson should have joined forces in demanding the installation, at Holmes's expense, of a fume-cupboard, with an outlet to the open air, to minimise the constant poisoning of the sitting-room atmosphere. However, there is no mention of this facility either and it was evidently not present. Nor, more importantly, is there any reference to Holmes's possession of a chemical balance, a *sine qua non* for chemical work of any kind.

In this connexion an extract from *The Copper Beeches* is not without interest.[2] "Holmes was settling down to one of those all-night researches which he frequently indulged in, when I would leave him stooping over a retort and test-tube at night, and find him in the same position when I came down to breakfast in the morning." This sounds like a *mise-en-scène*, or set-piece, staged solely for Watson's benefit. One pictures Holmes waiting until Watson had retired for the night, when he would follow suit, and rise in time to resume the tableau before Watson arrived for breakfast. However, on the present occasion the scene is interrupted by the receipt of a telegram summoning Holmes to Winchester, and he decides to "postpone [his] analysis of the acetones". This was perhaps fortunate, as it is hard to see how even the simplest analysis could have been performed without the aid of a chemical balance. Admittedly, the argument from silence is not wholly satisfactory, but it is curious, to say the least, that when so many vivid details are given in the stories about the furnishings and contents of the sitting-room, these three necessary items, particularly the sink and the balance, should nowhere be mentioned, even if only to deplore their absence.

Nevertheless, if these shortcomings did not prove insuperable, space would still be needed for other basic pieces of apparatus such as flasks, beakers, graduated jars, burettes, retort-stands and their attendant clamps of various sizes, a tripod stand and wire gauze, porcelain crucibles, funnels, filter-paper, glass and rubber tubing, glass rods, a blow-pipe, a pair of tongs, and all the other bits and pieces which tend to accumulate even in the

[1] *The Dying Detective, S.*, pp. 1000–1. [2] *S.*, pp. 284–5.

smallest laboratory. A "Do-it-yourself" Home Chemistry Kit, supposing one was then obtainable, would surely not satisfy Sherlock Holmes. Little wonder that, along with criminal relics, chemicals also strayed from time to time into the butter-dish, or were found in even less desirable places,[1] thus adding to the hazards of life at 221B.

We turn now from the apparatus to the use Holmes made of it. When we (and Watson) first encounter him he is engaged in chemical research in the laboratory of St. Bartholomew's Hospital, his own resources in Montague Street having evidently proved inadequate for his purpose. "I have found a reagent which is precipitated by haemoglobin, and by nothing else",[2] he declared in triumph—an extravagant claim if ever there was one, but not uncharacteristic. Another example of the same thing is Holmes's deduction that Watson had visited the Wigmore Street Post Office from the "little reddish mould" adhering to his instep. "Just opposite the Wigmore Street Office they have taken up the pavement and thrown up some earth, which lies in such a way that it is difficult to avoid treading in it in entering. The earth is of this peculiar reddish tint which is found, as far as I know, nowhere else in the neighbourhood."[3] Holmes's reasoning about the haemoglobin test, as about the reddish mould on Watson's instep, though qualified in the latter case by the words "as far as I know", rests on the fallacy of the undistributed middle. Both conclusions are therefore false in logic, though by a lucky chance they might prove correct in practice. But Holmes did not believe in luck. He relied on the observation of trifles and an encyclo-paedic memory.

The ingredients of the Sherlock Holmes test for haemoglobin were a drop of blood, a litre of water into which "he threw . . . a few white crystals", in the style of Mrs. Beeton, followed by "some drops of a transparent fluid". This produced a brownish precipitate. The demonstration would have been more impres-sive if it had been accompanied by a control experiment conducted without the drop of blood. The composition of the white crystals and also the transparent fluid remains a secret.

[1] *The Musgrave Ritual, S.,* p. 396.   [2] *A Study in Scarlet, L.,* pp. 9–11.
[3] *The Sign of Four, L.,* pp. 147–8.

In spite of Holmes's transports of delight at his discovery, which he anticipated would revolutionise criminal investigation involving either old or fresh bloodstains, there is no single instance of the use of his test in any subsequent case. Like Watson's bull-pup, mentioned on the same occasion, it vanishes into oblivion, never to be heard of again.

An interesting conversation between Holmes and Watson occurs in *A Case of Identity*.[1] Watson has returned to Baker Street after spending the day on a professional case of great gravity, to find Holmes half asleep in his armchair.

> "A formidable array of bottles and test-tubes, with the pungent cleanly smell of hydrochloric acid, told me that he had spent his whole day in the chemical work which was so dear to him.
> 'Well, have you solved it?' I asked as I entered.
> 'Yes. It was the bisulphate of baryta.'
> 'No, no, the mystery!' I cried.
> 'Oh, that! I thought of the salt that I have been working upon.' "

Baryta is the medical name generally given to barium sulphate. The good doctor may have imagined at this point that he was writing another prescription,—or perhaps we can detect here the hand of the Literary Agent. A chemist would normally have replied in the same circumstances, "Yes. It was barium bisulphate."

The smell of hydrochloric acid is certainly pungent in strong concentration. Whether it could also be described as "cleanly" is purely a matter of taste. The aroma in the room on this occasion may well have been an improvement upon the smells produced at some other times, after a day's chemical work by Holmes.

Reference has already been made to the apparatus mentioned in *The Naval Treaty*, and to the process of distillation and condensation which Holmes was somehow managing to càrry out without the aid of a supply of running cold water.[2] Watson arrives on the scene.

> "My friend hardly glanced up as I entered, and I, seeing that his investigation must be of importance, seated myself in an armchair and waited. He dipped into this bottle or that, drawing out a few

[1] *S.*, p. 69.

[2] *S.*, pp. 500–1.

drops of each with his glass pipette, and finally brought a test-tube containing a solution over to the table. In his right hand he had a slip of litmus paper.

'You come at a crisis, Watson', said he. 'If this paper remains blue, all is well. If it turns red, it means a man's life'. He dipped it into the test-tube, and it flushed at once into a dull, dirty crimson. 'Hum! I thought as much', he cried."

This is the only instance on record in which Holmes's chemical activities were directed towards the solution of one of his cases, albeit termed by him "a very commonplace little murder". We are, unfortunately, left in ignorance of the reason why an acid reaction to the litmus test proved the guilt of the murderer. The crime was evidently too commonplace to warrant inclusion in Dr. Watson's writings, though the chemical process by means of which it was solved would not have been without interest. History, therefore, fails to record whether the unsupported findings of an amateur chemist were admitted as evidence for the prosecution at the subsequent trial.

The case of *The Dancing Men* affords proof that Holmes did not always allow the claims of chemical research to outweigh those of hunger. He remarks, "If there is an afternoon train to town, Watson, I think we should do well to take it, as I have a chemical analysis of some interest to finish."[1] But later the same day he says, "Three-forty is our train, and I fancy we should be back in Baker Street for dinner."[2] First things first.

When we come to *His Last Bow* and *The Case-Book*, the chemical corner seems to have lost its attraction altogether, even in times of inactivity. After four fog-bound days, the first three of which Holmes had spent in cross-indexing his huge book of references, and in studying the music of the Middle Ages (a recent hobby), "he paced restlessly about our sitting-room in a fever of suppressed energy, biting his nails, tapping the furniture and chafing against inaction".[3] If he had been weaned from the seven per-cent cocaine solution at such moments of enforced idleness, it is clear also that he had ceased to find a substitute for it in chemical research. And towards the end of Holmes's career in Baker Street, Watson is no longer able to

[1] *S.*, pp. 629–30. [2] *Ibid.*, p. 638.
[3] *The Bruce-Partington Plans, S.*, p. 968.

include chemistry among his friend's interests. "He was a man of habits . . . and I had become one of them. As an institution I was like the violin, the shag tobacco, the old black pipe, the index-books, and others perhaps less excusable."[1]

In the interests of completing this record of Holmes's active chemical work, reference must be made to the months he said he had spent in "a research into the coal-tar derivatives . . . in a laboratory at Montpelier, in the south of France".[2] This was an extra-territorial activity during the "great hiatus", and had even less effect on his practice as a consulting detective than any of the experiments he conducted in his sitting-room at home.

With this exception, the following table gives the number of references to the actual performance of chemical work by Holmes, as they are distributed throughout the canon. It excludes mere statements about his interest in chemistry or the existence of equipment.

Long Stories.		2.	A Study in Scarlet
			The Sign of Four
Short Stories.	Adventures.	2.	A Case of Identity
			The Copper Beeches
	Memoirs.	2.	The "Gloria Scott"
			The Naval Treaty
	Return.	1.	The Dancing Men
	His Last Bow.	Nil	
	The Case-Book.	Nil	

This table demonstrates that the façade of chemical research, never very strong, became less and less well-maintained as time went on, until it collapsed entirely. The back-cloth of chemical apparatus and equipment—the chemical corner—was, however, kept in being up to the end of the Baker Street tenancy. There is nothing to show that it was transferred to Holmes's final retreat on the Sussex Downs. True, in *The Final Problem* he looks forward to a time when, as he says, "I could continue to live in the quiet fashion which is most congenial to me, and to concentrate my attention upon my chemical researches."[3]

[1] *The Creeping Man, S.,* p. 1244.   [2] *The Empty House, S.,* p. 569.
[3] *S.,* p. 539.

But in *The Abbey Grange* he proposes to devote his declining years to the composition of a text-book focussing the whole art of detection into one volume.[1] So far, no proof has come to light that either of these ambitions was ever fulfilled. What Holmes did do, in the event, was to write his *magnum opus* on the subject of bee-keeping, namely the *Practical Handbook of Bee Culture, with some Observations upon the Segregation of the Queen,* described in *His Last Bow* as a small blue book, with the title printed in golden letters across the cover.[2]

Three final extracts, from the first two long stories, provide a clue to the *raison d'être* of the chemical corner.

> "Like all other arts, the Science of Deduction and Analysis is one which can only be acquired by long and patient study, nor is life long enough to allow any mortal to attain the highest possible perfection in it."[3]
>
> "Detection is, or ought to be, an exact science, and should be treated in the same cold and unemotional manner."[4]
>
> "My mind . . . rebels at stagnation. Give me problems, give me work, give me the most abstruse cryptogram, or the most intricate analysis, and I am in my proper atmosphere. I can dispense then with artificial stimulants."[5]

We may conclude, therefore, that the main purpose of Holmes's chemical corner was to keep him in practical touch with an exact science where cause and effect, action and reaction, followed each other with a predictability beyond the power of the less precise "science of detection" to achieve, however hard he might strive towards exactitude in his chosen profession. His chemical experiments were designed neither to advance the sum of human knowledge, nor his own career. They were purely a solace to his spirit. When he was marooned "for some weeks in one of our great University towns", Watson said of him "My friend's temper had not improved since he had been deprived of the congenial surroundings of Baker Street. Without his scrap-books, his chemicals, and his homely untidiness, he was an uncomfortable man."[6]

Two subsidiary purposes, perhaps, also came to be served by

[1] *S.*, p. 834.
[2] *S.*, pp. 1079–80.
[3] *A Study in Scarlet, L.*, p. 20.
[4] *The Sign of Four, L.*, p. 145.
[5] *Ibid., L.*, p. 144.
[6] *The Three Students, S.*, pp. 763–4.

the chemical corner. It helped to mystify Watson, a pursuit in which Holmes always seemed to take a somewhat perverse delight. Also he might anticipate that the array of bottles, and such chemical apparatus as there was, would instil confidence into the mind of the client as he, or she, gazed nervously around the Baker Street sitting-room. Here, obviously, were the outward signs of a man of wide knowledge and experience who could be trusted to analyse and solve a human problem with the same scientific and deductive skills as he would bring to bear on a problem in chemistry. The barest minimum of equip-r.ent would suffice to set the scene for the casual visitor, who, for his part, would be unlikely to notice that its deficiencies were such as to render the performance of serious chemical work impracticable, if not impossible.

IV

POINTS NORTH

by the Venerable Charles O. Ellison

I T was on the occasion of his first meeting with Sir Henry
Baskerville, and in the presence of Dr. James Mortimer and
Watson, that Holmes remarked: "I confess that once when I
was very young I confused the *Leeds Mercury* with the *Western
Morning News.*"[1] Does this confession encourage us to be-
lieve that Holmes once paid a professional visit to Yorkshire?

The first question to be decided is which of the two papers it
actually was. A careful perusal of the wording favours the view
that Holmes was confronted with the first-named paper—the
Leeds Mercury—which is the object of the verb "confused". If
one says "I mistook A for B", the plain meaning is that it was,
in fact, A, and not B. If one adopts the less precise form "I
confused A with B," the meaning is still the same though
perhaps not quite so instantly clear as before. We may therefore
conclude with every confidence that Holmes was presented with
an extract from the *Leeds Mercury* which at first he thought had
come from the *Western Morning News.* His statement could be
expanded to read "I confused the *Leeds Mercury* (which indeed
it was) with the *Western Morning News* (which it was not) and
later discovered my mistake".

The *Leeds Mercury,* subsequently absorbed in the *Yorkshire
Post,* circulated during its long life as an independent newspaper
mainly in Leeds, and also to a limited extent further afield in

[1] *The Hound of the Baskervilles, L.,* p. 305.

the West Riding. However, it was essentially a local paper. The *Western Morning News* was, and still is, published in Plymouth, and has a wide circulation in the West Country. In common with the more important publications of the Provincial Press both papers had London offices, and these were within a few doors of each other in Fleet Street.

At the risk of stressing the obvious, one must assume that all that Holmes had before him when he confused the two papers was a mere fragment of newsprint, providing no clue as to its provenance beyond the characteristics of the type-face. No confusion could arise when he was studying differences of newspaper type in the course of preparing himself for his future career as the world's first consulting detective, for he would then be handling complete newspapers, and would only have to turn to the front page, or the top of any page, to find out which paper he was looking at. He himself observed "the detection of types is one of the most elementary branches of knowledge to the special expert in crime".[1] We may be sure therefore that the subject was not neglected, and indeed could have been conveniently studied when, at the very outset of his career, he was living in "rooms in Montague Street, just round the corner from the British Museum".[2]

One would like to think that the fragment of newsprint was a clue in a very early case—"when I was very young"—but more of this later. We may also surmise that it consisted of separate words cut out of the paper and pasted on to a sheet to form an anonymous message in the style of the warning message in *The Hound of the Baskervilles* which prompted the reminiscent confession, and which in the light of Holmes's greater experience was at once identified as being taken from a *Times* leader. A complete paragraph would have been more readily identifiable, and traced to its source with less chance of mistake. The bigger the cutting the easier the problem, for additional features such as width of column, quality of paper, local allusions, and even, provided the specimen were large enough, the general editorial layout, would all then come to the assistance of the investigator.

The year of *The Hound of the Baskervilles* is canonically

---

[1] *The Hound of the Baskervilles*, L., p. 305.
[2] *The Musgrave Ritual*, S., p. 399.

inferred to be 1889 (i.e. five years after the date—1884—
inscribed on Dr. Mortimer's walking stick).[1] This date, for
various reasons, is disputed by critics in favour of later years
up to, and including, 1899. If Holmes had been born in 1854
(in order to be 60 in 1914),[2] he would be between 35 and 45
years of age when he made the confession about the *Leeds
Mercury*. What period of his life is conjured up by those words
"once when I was very young"? Was he alluding to his school-
days some 20 or 30 years before, according to the date attributed to the *Hound*, or to his University days, say five years
later, or to the earliest days of his professional practice starting
some three years after that?

A temporary misjudgment in identifying the source of a
fragment of newspaper, occurring at school, when the exercise
of his growing powers of deduction would be little more than
a spare-time recreation, is not at all likely to have made such a
lasting impression as to be recalled, not without shame, 20 or
30 years afterwards. An almost impenetrable veil is drawn over
Holmes's boyhood and school-life. All we can safely conclude is
that, descended as he was from a line of country squires, his
formative years were passed in the country, (where he acquired
a lasting interest in bee-keeping) possibly in East Sussex, to
which he returned in his retirement. But that is all. Baring-
Gould has a fanciful theory that the youthful Holmes was taught
for a time by a tutor (whom he identified as Moriarty) at his
home in a hill-side farmstead named Mycroft, situated in the
village of Sigerside in the North Riding of Yorkshire.[3] Although
such a setting would bring him within 70 miles or so of the
district in which the *Leeds Mercury* circulated, the whole idea
must be rejected out of hand if only for the good reason that no
such places as Mycroft and Sigerside exist, outside Baring-
Gould's imagination.

Turning now to Holmes's time at the University, and firmly
resisting any attempt to decide between the rival claims of
Oxford and Cambridge, we find that whilst his few acquaintances
had already noticed, and indeed talked about "those habits of
observation and inference which [he] had already formed into

---

[1] *The Hound of the Baskervilles, L.*, p. 275.
[2] *His Last Bow, S.*, p. 1076.   [3] *op. cit.*, pp. 16–20.

a system"[1] there was as yet no thought in his own mind that they were to form the basis of his future career. They remained, as he put it, "the merest hobby".[2] Any sustained course of study in preparation for that career had to be postponed until he had left the University for the rooms in Montague Street where he "waited, filling in [his] too abundant leisure time by studying all those branches of science which might make [him] more efficient",[3] including, as has been suggested, the ability to distinguish at a glance between various type-faces. This must surely be the period when a failure to apply the fruits of his long hours in the British Museum, and correctly identify a newspaper by its type, would rankle in his mind and not be easily forgotten.

If it be objected that only some 20 years at the most had elapsed between the Montague Street days and his involvement with *The Hound of the Baskervilles*, and therefore "once when I was very young" might appear somewhat exaggerated language, it may well be thought that Holmes meant to describe himself as having been at the time "very young" in experience rather than in years.

To a Yorkshireman like myself it would be attractive to think that Holmes, in one of his early, pre-Watson, cases, operated, if only for a day or two, in the neighbourhood of the city of Leeds. If he did so, one may be permitted to hope that after his mistaken identification of the piece, or pieces, of newspaper, he resisted the temptation to catch the first train from Leeds to Devonshire (The Devonian?)—no doubt even then waiting in the Wellington Station with steam up—under the impression that the vital fragment of newsprint emanated from Plymouth.

However, it must be conceded that copies of the *Leeds Mercury* would not be confined only to Leeds and its vicinity. They could have turned up almost anywhere. Travellers from Leeds to King's Cross or St. Pancras would buy the paper to read on the journey, and leave it behind in the train to be picked up by any railway employee or casual passer-by. The paper would often serve to wrap or pack goods destined for all parts of the country. Casual sales of both the *Leeds Mercury* and the

[1] *The 'Gloria Scott'*, S., p. 376. [2] *Ibid.*, p. 378.
[3] *The Musgrave Ritual*, S., p. 399.

Western Morning News would be made from time to time at their respective London offices, as well as at railway bookstalls and other places far from their natural habitat.

When all is said and done, the confusion whereby a few snippets from the *Leeds Mercury* were at first thought to have come from the *Western Morning News* is far more likely to have arisen in Devonshire than in the West Riding. Confronted with some odd words cut from a newspaper, what is more natural than to suppose they have been taken from a local publication? That they were ultimately traced to a provincial paper circulating more than 300 miles away is an early feather in the deerstalker of the Master.

Of course, if the inference that Holmes was examining words from the *Leeds Mercury* which at first he took to have come from the *Western Morning News* is incorrect, and the reverse was the truth, then the confusion would have been more likely to occur in Leeds or its surroundings. But any argument based on this supposition would in my opinion be a weak one. Though the form of his confession is less clear than one would wish, it does logically favour the opposite view expressed at the start of this little essay.

On more than one occasion Holmes's work took him into the West Country. But there are only two cases, one definitely and the other potentially, which entailed a journey to the north in any real sense of the term. One of them, *The Priory School*, was duly recorded by Watson, and the other was unrecorded, being one of those cases "all done prematurely", as Holmes observes, "before my biographer had come to glorify me".[1] The first took him to the Derbyshire Peak District, and the second is the case of the Tarleton murders, the record of which he lifted from a large tin box "a third full of bundles of paper tied up with red tape into separate packages".[2] The use of the plural "murders" indicates beyond doubt that Tarleton is a place name and not a family name, and indeed it is the name of a village in West Lancashire, about 8 miles inland from Southport, which is a favourite holiday resort for Yorkshire folk. It is therefore an area into which the *Leeds Mercury* might well have found its way fairly frequently. However, Lancashire is

[1] *The Musgrave Ritual*, S., p. 397. [2] *Ibid.*, S., p. 397.

not Yorkshire. Although it is faintly possible that "The Tarleton murders" was the case in which the paper figured as a clue, it happened whilst Holmes was in his middle twenties—hardly an age to be described as "once when I was very young" by anyone other than a very senior citizen, unless, as already suggested, he meant "very young" in experience.

So the clue of the *Leeds Mercury*, at first sight a promising pointer in the desired direction, has proved, on examination, to lead nowhere in particular, and must be regretfully discarded as irrelevant in helping us to decide whether Holmes was ever consulted by a client from Yorkshire. It would also appear that the palm for providing the most northerly point reached in his professional travels must be awarded to Lancashire,—unless the Tarleton case followed the usual pattern of events in the early days and was solved by Holmes without leaving Montague Street. An exchange from *A Study in Scarlet* reveals his methods at that time.

Holmes (speaking of his clients): "I listen to their story, they listen to my comments, and then I pocket my fee."
Watson: "But do you mean to say that without leaving your room you can unravel some knot which other men can make nothing of, although they have seen every detail for themselves?"
Holmes: "Quite so. I have a kind of intuition that way. Now and again a case turns up which is a little more complex. Then I have to bustle about and see things with my own eyes."[1]

Let us hope that the careful preservation of the record of the Tarleton murders in the large tin box, tied up with red tape along with other papers, means that it was one of those cases in which Holmes had to go and view things for himself. But it is all very disappointing for the Yorkshire Sherlockian.[2]

[1] *A Study in Scarlet, L.*, p. 22.
[2] For Holmes's attitude to points further north in Scotland, see p. 11–12.

V

THOMAS STEARNS ELIOT AND
SHERLOCK HOLMES[1]

O N 13 July, 1953, a member of the Danish Sherlock Holmes
Club, A. D. Henriksen, wrote to T. S. Eliot (1888–1965),
the poet, essayist and playwright, to ask if it was true that he
had at some time written an article or essay on Sherlock Holmes.[2]
If Mr. Henriksen had looked in the one place that would have
answered his question, Donald Gallup's *T. S. Eliot. A Bibliography*, published in the previous year, he would have discovered
on p. 97 the entry for "Sherlock Holmes and His Times", a
signed essay contributed by Eliot to *The Criterion* of April,
1929. Ostensibly a review of the first collected edition of the
Sherlock Holmes short stories published by John Murray, it
was in fact an amusing piece of literary criticism, five pages in
length, demonstrating an understandable devotion to Sherlock
Holmes and a close acquaintance with the literature of Baker
Street.

Dr. Eliot replied immediately to Mr. Henriksen's letter on
16 July, 1953, using the letterheading of Messrs. Faber &

[1] This chapter is an adaptation of a talk delivered by me at the conclusion of my
Presidential Address to the Annual General Meeting of the Leeds Library on
10 April, 1972. Its theme and contents were recorded in our published Annual
Report for 1972. It owes nothing, therefore, to the essay "Two Napoleons of
Crime. A Comparison between T. S. Eliot's Macavity and Sir Arthur Conan
Doyle's Moriarty", by E. Hamill, published in February, 1973, in *The Sherlock
Holmes Journal*, Winter, 1972, ii, No. 1.

[2] The correspondence was recorded by Mr. Henriksen in *The Sherlock Holmes
Journal*, Winter, 1965, viii, No. 3.

Faber, the publishing firm of which he was a director, in the following terms:

> "Dear Sir,
>
> I thank you for your letter of July 13th, and am very sorry to have to inform you that I have never written an essay such as you mention, nor in spite of my admiration for Sherlock Holmes have I ever written any essay or paper on the subject. I have always, however, been a devoted supporter."

It may be thought that the evidence is conflicting. On the one hand we have Dr. Eliot's flat denial of ever having written anything. On the other we have the actual five-page essay in *The Criterion*, signed "T. S. Eliot" and faithfully recorded by his bibliographer in 1952. It may, of course, be urged that literary forgery is not unknown, but in the matter of the essay "Sherlock Holmes and His Times" it must be conceded that even the most skilful of forgers would have experienced difficulty in getting a faked essay signed "T. S. Eliot" printed in *The Criterion* in 1929. According to his entries in *Who's Who*, the Editor of *The Criterion* at that time was T. S. Eliot himself.

More seriously, I would say that in this admirable piece of writing about Sherlock Holmes, Eliot established his position among the earliest of the Higher Critics of the subject, closely following Monsignor Ronald Knox's "Studies in the Literature of Sherlock Holmes", printed in permanent and generally accessible form in *Essays in Satire* in 1928.[1] Eliot, indeed, said in 1929 that whilst it might seem that Ronald Knox had said the last word on Sherlock Holmes, he had in fact overlooked several interesting points. One example of Eliot's innocent queries was on the matter of capital punishment in the Victorian era, suggested by the remark of John Clay in *The Red-Headed League*, "I'll swing for it!", when caught robbing the Coburg branch of the City and Suburban Bank. Of the same incident Eliot also expressed wonderment over the fashions in garments worn by burglars digging tunnels under banks at that period, since Inspector Athelney Jones was able to tear off the coat-tails of Clay's frock-coated accomplice.[2] But at the end of these and

---

[1] The essay first appeared in *The Oxford Blue Book*, in 1912.
[2] *The Red-Headed League*, S., p. 52.

other sallies in 1929 Eliot paid the Holmes saga one of the most graceful compliments of any commentator before or since:

> "And yet, if all the contemporary detective story writers brought out new books at the same time, and one of them was a new Holmes, it is the Holmes that we should read first."

Eliot said that "every writer owes something to Holmes", adding:

> "And every critic of The Novel who has a theory about the reality of characters in fiction, would do well to consider Holmes . . . I am not sure that Sir Arthur Conan Doyle is not one of the great dramatic writers of his age."

And of Doyle and his most famous creation, Eliot wrote with great insight:

> "Another, and perhaps the greatest of the Sherlock Holmes mysteries is this: that when we talk of him we invariably fall into the fancy of his existence. Collins, after all is more real to his readers than Cuff; Poe is more real than Dupin; but Sir Arthur Conan Doyle, the eminent spiritualist, the author of a number of exciting stories which we read years ago and have forgotten, what has he to do with Holmes?"

That Eliot was devoted to Sherlock Holmes and constantly paid homage to him is evident from many of his writings, a fact which two or three examples will demonstrate. In 1939 his *Old Possum's Book of Practical Cats* was published by Faber and Faber. It was a witty collection of light verse, memorable for its brilliant observation of cat-life and the resemblance that exists between cats and certain types of humans. It included a poem of 42 lines, "Macavity: The Mystery Cat."[1] It is not difficult to show that Eliot's description of Macavity is simply that of Dr. James Moriarty, the master-criminal of the Holmes adventures of *The Final Problem* and *The Valley of Fear*. Let us look, for example, at lines 11, 12, 13 and 15 containing Eliot's account of Macavity's physical appearance:

> "Macavity's a ginger cat, he's very tall and thin;
> You would know him if you saw him, for his eyes are sunken in.
> His brow is deeply lined with thought, his head is highly domed . . .

[1] *Old Possum's Book of Practical Cats* (London, 1939), pp. 33–5.

He sways his head from side to side, with movements like a
snake."

This can be compared with Holmes's description to Watson
of Dr. Moriarty, precisely similar, it may be thought, even to
the odd snake-like movement of the head:

> "He is extremely tall and thin, his forehead domes out in a white
> curve, and his two eyes are deeply sunken in his head . . . His face
> protrudes forward, and is for ever slowly oscillating from side to
> side in a curiously reptilian fashion."[1]

Eliot's description gives the impression that if we could see
Macavity and Moriarty together we would hardly be able to
distinguish one from the other, apart from the fact, perhaps,
that Moriarty was clean-shaven and Macavity, like most cats,
was not.

Both Macavity and Moriarty followed the same profession.
Eliot's opening lines were:

> "Macavity's a Mystery Cat: he's called the Hidden Paw—
> For he's the master criminal who can defy the Law.
> He's the bafflement of Scotland Yard, the Flying Squad's despair:
> For when they reach the scene of crime—*Macavity's not there!*"

The theme that Macavity did not actually take any physical
part in crimes he organised is a constant one, and the phrase
"Macavity's not there", with slight variations, was repeated
seven times throughout the poem. In lines 38 to 42 Eliot made
the complementary point that Macavity used agents:-

> "At whatever time the deed took place—MACAVITY WASN'T
> THERE!
> And they say that all the Cats whose wicked deeds are widely
> known
> (I might mention Mungojerrie, I might mention Griddlebone)
> Are nothing more than agents for the Cat who all the time,
> Just controls their operations: the Napoleon of Crime!"

Holmes said of Moriarty:

> "He is the Napoleon of crime, Watson. He is the organizer of half
> that is evil and of nearly all that is undetected in this great city . . .
> He does little himself. He only plans. But his agents are numerous

[1] *The Final Problem, S.,* p. 541.

48

and splendidly organized. Is there a crime to be done, a paper to be abstracted, we will say, a house to be rifled, a man to be removed— the word is passed to the Professor, the matter is organized and carried out. The agent may be caught. In that case money is found for his bail or his defence. But the central power which uses the agent is never caught—never so much as suspected."[1]

On this same theme of the use of agents and the master criminal's prudent absence from the scene of the crime, it will be remembered that Moriarty was a mathematician. In the case of *The Final Problem*, when Holmes was telling Watson how he had been attacked by one of Moriarty's agents, armed with a bludgeon, he said:

"I knocked him down, and the police have him in custody; but I can tell you with the most absolute confidence that no possible connection will ever be traced between the gentleman upon whose front teeth I have barked my knuckles and the retiring mathematical coach, who is, I dare say, working out problems upon a blackboard ten miles away."[2]

We may compare this passage from *The Final Problem* with lines 31 to 34 of *Macavity*, in which the similar safety from the law by reason of distance from the scene of the crime and a pre-occupation with mathematics, are both emphasised:

"And when the loss has been disclosed, the Secret Service say:
'It *must* have been Macavity!'—but he's a mile away.
You'll be sure to find him resting, or a-licking of his thumbs,
Or engaged in doing complicated long division sums."

Lines 27 and 28 of *Macavity* give two examples of the kind of crimes organised by the feline master-criminal:

"And when the Foreign Office find a Treaty's gone astray,
Or the Admiralty lose some plans and drawings by the way . . .".

These phrases cannot help but remind us of the Sherlock Holmes adventures of *The Naval Treaty*, in which the top-secret document defining the position of Great Britain towards the Triple Alliance disappeared from the Foreign Office, and *The Bruce-Partington Plans*, in which the vital drawings of a revolutionary

---

[1] *The Final Problem, S.*, p. 540. [2] *Ibid., S.*, p. 544.

submarine, the most jealously guarded of all British naval secrets, were stolen.

Eliot said on line 21 that Macavity was "outwardly respectable". In *The Valley of Fear* Holmes told Watson that Moriarty's outward-seeming respectability, as "the celebrated author of *The Dynamics of an Asteroid*" was such that in calling him a criminal Watson was "uttering libel in the eyes of the law, and there lies the glory and wonder of it".[1] Holmes used a similar phrase in *The Final Problem*, when he exclaimed of Moriarty to Watson:

> "Aye, there's the genius and the wonder of the thing!" he cried. "The man pervades London, and no one has heard of him."[2]

The first sentence of Eliot's line 26 was nearly a quotation of Holmes, just as "The Napoleon of Crime"[3] was an exact one.

> "Aye, there's the wonder of the thing! *Macavity's not there!*"

One phrase of Eliot's about Macavity on line 21, "They say he cheats at cards", was not applicable to Dr. Moriarty, so far as we know. Oddly enough, however, it was precisely descriptive of his deputy Colonel Sebastian Moran, who shot the Hon. Ronald Adair with an expanding bullet from an air-gun through the open window of the second floor front of No. 427 Park Lane. Holmes told Watson:

> "Now, Moran undoubtedly played foul—of that I have long been aware. I believe that on the day of the murder, Adair had discovered that Moran was cheating. Very likely he had spoken to him privately, and had threatened to expose him unless he voluntarily resigned his membership of the club and promised not to play cards again . . . The exclusion from his clubs would mean ruin to Moran, who lived by his ill-gotten card gains."[4]

If we think that Eliot's memory was occasionally unreliable, in that in 1953, for example, he had entirely forgotten that he had ever written an essay on Sherlock Holmes, it may seem to us possible that he confused Moriarty with Moran in the matter of cheating at cards. On the other hand, two lines in Eliot's

---

[1] *The Valley of Fear*, L., p. 460.   [2] *The Final Problem*, S., pp. 538–9.
[3] One wonders why the admiring Watson never responded by suggesting that Holmes was the Wellington of detection.
[4] *The Empty House*, S., pp. 582–3.

poem "Gus: The Theatre Cat", which immediately follows "Macavity" in *Old Possum's Book of Practical Cats*, suggest that his memory of other aspects of Colonel Moran's life was very clear indeed. The lines are:

> "He once played a Tiger—could do it again—
> Which an Indian Colonel pursued down a drain."

Holmes described Colonel Moran to Watson as "the best shot in India" and remarked of him, "He was always a man of iron nerve, and the story is still told in India of how he crawled down a drain after a wounded man-eating tiger".[1]

Touches of Sherlock Holmes appear in many of Eliot's poems. One of the most interesting, from the point of view of the textual critic, occurs in his "East Coker", which first appeared in *The New English Weekly* in 1940 and then, in company with "Burnt Norton", "The Dry Salvages" and "Little Gidding", in *Four Quartets*, published in 1944. The significant lines are:

> "In the middle, not only in the middle of the way.
> But all the way, in a dark wood, in a bramble,
> On the edge of a grimpen, where is no secure foothold."

What, we may reasonably ask, is a "grimpen"? The word is not contained either in the *Concise Oxford Dictionary*, nor in *Chambers's Twentieth Century Dictionary*, nor is it even to be found in the row of massive all-embracing volumes of the *OED*, the *New English Dictionary on Historical Principles*, edited originally by Sir J. A. H. Murray and others and published by the Oxford University Press. It can be said, therefore, that as a common noun "grimpen" does not exist in the English language.

Yet Eliot used it. He used it in his metaphor to mean some physical hazard which could exist, in this case within the precincts of a dark wood, into which the traveller might sink or fall, since there was no secure foothold. It is of great interest, therefore, to recall Dr. Watson's first meeting with Stapleton, the naturalist, during a walk on the moor in the seventh chapter of *The Hound of the Baskervilles*. Stapleton introduced himself

---

[1] *The Empty House*, S., pp. 579–80.

and described some of the features of the moor, and in particular a great plain of land with queer hills protruding from it:

" 'You notice those bright green spots scattered thickly over it?' 'Yes, they seem more fertile than the rest'.
Stapleton laughed. 'That is the great Grimpen Mire', said he. 'A false step yonder means death to man or beast. Only yesterday I saw one of the moor ponies wander into it. He never came out'."[1]

It may be thought that any doubt as to whether T. S. Eliot had read and remembered *The Hound of the Baskervilles* is removed by his "Lines to Ralph Hodgson, Esquire", a short poem which originally appeared in *The Criterion* of January, 1933, and was later published in 1936 in his *Collected Poems* 1909–1935. The relevant lines are:

"How delightful to meet Mr. Hodgson!
(Everyone wants to know *him*)
With his musical sound
And his Baskerville Hound
Which, just at a word from his master,
Will follow you faster and faster,
And tear you limb from limb".

I turn for my final example to T. S. Eliot's *Murder in the Cathedral*, first published in 1935, and to the first six lines of the dialogue between Thomas à Becket and the Second Tempter. The questions are asked by Thomas and answered by the Tempter, who is urging the archbishop to submit to the King's will, and thus recover the Chancellorship and exercise temporal power for the good of the kingdom.

"Whose was it?
His who is gone.
Who shall have it?
He who will come.
What shall be the month?
The last from the first."

These six lines can be compared with those of the questions and answers of *The Musgrave Ritual*, a mystery which was the central theme of one of Holmes's earliest cases, and was first published in *The Strand Magazine* in May, 1893. He was

[1] *The Hound of the Baskervilles*, L., p. 343.

consulted, it will be remembered, by Reginald Musgrave, with whom he had been up at Cambridge. The first six lines of the Ritual were:

> "Whose was it?
> His who is gone.
> Who shall have it?
> He who will come.
> What was the month?
> The sixth from the first".[1]

It will be seen that the six lines quoted from *Murder in the Cathedral* are identical with those in *The Musgrave Ritual*, with the exception of only three words.

It will be recalled that Brunton, the unusual butler of the Manor House at Hurlstone, the ancestral home of the Musgraves, was led by his unscrupulous curiosity and high intelligence to unravel the mystery of the strange catechism to which each Musgrave had to submit when he came to man's estate. Brunton divined that the ancient Ritual was the clue to the hiding-place of a treasure, including the lost crown of King Charles I, and his attempt to steal it cost him his life. The connexion between this tragedy and that of *Murder in the Cathedral* is perhaps less tenuous than it seems. The crown which once encircled the brows of the Royal Stuarts, which Brunton found by deciphering the Ritual, signified the secular power of the Kings of England. *The Musgrave Ritual* was therefore an account of the attempted recovery of a symbol of dominion, which may be thought to have points of similarity with what was offered to Thomas à Becket by the Second Tempter.

I am not the first critic to compare *The Musgrave Ritual* with *Murder in the Cathedral*, but I hope that I am the first writer to assemble most of the facts and publish them in permanent form. So far as I know, the first mention of the matter occurred in an essay by Miss Elizabeth Jackson published in 1941.[1] Little notice seems to have been taken of the paragraph Miss Jackson devoted to it, and in 1948 Mr. Grover Smith of Yale University

---

[1] *The Musgrave Ritual*, S., p. 407.
[2] "Poetry and Poppycock", *The Saturday Review of Literature*, 25 January, 1941, pp. 13–14.

published the discovery in *Notes and Queries*.[1] Three years later, in a letter to *The Times Literary Supplement*, Professor Alan Clutton-Brock also innocently claimed to have discovered the startling similarity between the lines in *Murder in the Cathedral* and *The Musgrave Ritual*.[2] A letter followed, however, in the same month from Professor Jacob Isaacs pointing out the previous publication of the matter by Mr. Grover Smith.[3] Interestingly enough, this imbroglio was finally disentangled by a Sherlock Holmes enthusiast, Mr. Nathan Bengis of New York. Mr. Bengis was not entirely convinced by one theory, originally advanced by Miss Elizabeth Jackson, that early familiarity with the Sherlock Holmes stories had caused these lines merely to drop into the well, so to speak, of Eliot's sub-conscious. After referring to the correspondence that had appeared in *The Times Literary Supplement* earlier in 1951, Mr. Bengis said in a letter published in that periodical:

> "Remembering Sherlock Holmes's warning about the danger of theorizing before one has all the evidence, I wrote to Mr. Eliot in May of this year and asked him about the matter point-blank. I quote with permission from his reply. 'My use of The Musgrave Ritual was deliberate and wholly conscious'. This definitive answer should, I think, end the discussion of this much-mooted point."[4]

Mr. Grover-Smith concluded his letter to *The Times Literary Supplement* in 1948 with the remark, "It is agreeable that the achievements of our most distinguished detective should have contributed to Eliot's work". I would add that T. S. Eliot can be numbered among those included by inference in his own assertion in *The Criterion* in 1929, already quoted in this essay, that every writer owes something to Sherlock Holmes. For the lover of the magic of Baker Street, it must be a matter of pleasure that one of the greatest of modern men of letters was so clearly devoted to Sherlock Holmes, and repeatedly paid homage in his published work to the memory of the great consulting detective.

[1] "T. S. Eliot and Sherlock Holmes", *Notes and Queries*, 2 October, 1948, pp. 431–2.
[2] *TLS*, 19 January, 1951, p. 37.   [3] *TLS*, 26 January, 1951, p. 53.
[4] *TLS*, 28 September, 1951, p. 613.

VI

SHERLOCK HOLMES AND ARSÈNE LUPIN

IN the penultimate paragraph of "Sherlock Holmes and His Times" T. S. Eliot wrote:

"And France, in the person of Arsène Lupin (about whom I hope to write at length) has rendered homage to him. What greater compliment could France pay to England than the scene in which the two great antagonists, Holmes and Lupin, are lying side by side on deckchairs on the Calais–Dover paquebot, and the London Commissioner of Police walks up and down the deck unsuspecting."[1]

If Eliot ever did write an essay on the very worthwhile subject of Arsène Lupin, the great French gentleman-burglar and supreme master of disguise, whose adventures were recorded by Maurice Emile Leblanc (1864–1941)[2] early in the present century, I have been unable to trace any reference to it in Donald Gallup's *T. S. Eliot. A Bibliography* or elsewhere. It is, however, of great interest that Eliot referred to the great detective in the French setting of the Lupin stories as Holmes, and not as "Holmlock Shears", the thinly disguised pseudonym

[1] *The Criterion*, April, 1929, p. 556.
[2] Leblanc was born in Rouen, of Franco-Italian descent. His sister, the actress Georgette Leblanc, was for many years the companion of Maurice Maeterlinck, who wrote several of his plays for her. Just as ardent Sherlockians toy with the idea that Sir Arthur Conan Doyle's knighthood in 1902 and the publication of *The Hound of the Baskervilles* in *The Strand Magazine* from August, 1901–April, 1902 was no mere coincidence, so some may see a similar connexion between Maurice Leblanc's ribbon of the Legion of Honour and his recording of the adventures of Arsène Lupin. The assertion by Willard Huntington Wright ("S. S. Van Dine") in *The World's Great Detective Stories* that Leblanc's death occurred in 1926 is erroneous. He died at Perpignan on 6 November, 1941. The copyright of his work is owned by Claude Leblanc.

generally used by Leblanc. According to the report of an interview with Leblanc's son, printed in the *Magazine Littéraire* in May, 1971, his father originally used the name "Sherlock Holmes", but modified it slightly at the request of Conan Doyle. Be that as it may, there can be no doubt about Leblanc's admiration for the great Englishman, as was made clear by his warm tribute to Doyle on the occasion of the latter's death.[1] I shall follow T. S. Eliot's example in the pages that follow by avoiding the use of "Holmlock Shears", except in quoting the actual titles of publications.

Ellery Queen quoted the second of Eliot's two sentences in his introduction to the Lupin episode, "Holmlock Shears Arrives Too Late", which he included in his collection of Sherlockian pastiches and parodies, adding:

> "[Holmes] is the only detective whom Leblanc considered a worthy adversary for his clever and resourceful Arsène. For while Lupin consistantly vanquished Ganimard, Guerchard and all the other Gallic sleuths, he never achieved more than a draw against the great Englishman—a monumental tribute indeed from that true French gentleman, M. Leblanc, who for a time controlled the destiny of Britain's man of the ages."[2]

Leblanc confirmed this opinion of the graceful balance of power when he wrote of "these two men, both so out of the common, so powerfully armed, both really superior characters, and inevitably destined by their special aptitudes to come into collision, like two equal forces which the order of things drives one against the other in space", in "Holmlock Shears Arrives Too Late".[3]

Since both Ellery Queen and T. S. Eliot have conceded that the subject of Sherlock Holmes in the context of Arsène Lupin is worthy of study,[4] and because Leblanc's books are now hard to find, an examination of some of the problems presented by the relevant literature may be appropriate. Queen rightly points out that only three of the Lupin episodes involve Sherlock

---

[1] "A propos de Conan Doyle", *Les Annales Politiques et Littéraires*, August, 1930. This essay has recently been translated by Dr. Kai-Ho Mai, and published in *The Baker Street Journal*, June, 1971, xxi, No. 2, pp. 100–3. In it Leblanc referred warmly to Conan Doyle as his friend.
[2] *The Misadventures of Sherlock Holmes* (Boston, 1944), p. 15.
[3] *Ibid.*, p. 30.
[4] It has not been attempted before, so far as I am aware.

Holmes, so that the field of investigation is conveniently restricted. These were, in the order in which Queen lists them and with his dates, "Holmlock Shears Arrives Too Late", one of the adventures in the collection *The Exploits of Arsène Lupin* (New York, 1907), and the two full-length novels, *Arsène Lupin versus Holmlock Shears* (London, 1909) and *The Hollow Needle* (London, 1911).

I do not challenge this bibliographical information, other than to remark that *The English Catalogue of Books* records an edition of *The Hollow Needle* published in January, 1910, thus preceding the date of my copy, published in London by Eveleigh Nash in 1911, which for some time I assumed to be the date of the first English edition.[1] The earliest English version of *The Exploits of Arsène Lupin* recorded in *The English Catalogue* was that of 1908, published under the title of *The Seven of Hearts*.[2] Both *The English Catalogue* and *The British Museum Catalogue* confirm Ellery Queen's date of 1909 for the first English translation of *Arsène Lupin versus Holmlock Shears*, of which I possess the second edition published by Eveleigh Nash in 1911 under the title of *The Arrest of Arsène Lupin*.

It will be seen that I do not dispute Ellery Queen's sequence of publication of the three vital stories, and this is indeed confirmed by the dates of the original French editions. These were *Arsène Lupin, gentleman-cambrioleur* (Paris, 1907), *Arsène Lupin contre Herlock Sholmes* (Paris, 1908) and *L'Aiguille creuse* (Paris, 1909). I do not think, however, that we need assume, as Queen evidently does, that the dates of the adventures themselves necessarily follow the same order. Queen remarks that "the opening skirmish occurred . . . in 'Holmlock Shears Arrives Too Late'—that we now bring you". He considers that the events described in *Arsène Lupin versus Holmlock Shears* were "the further development of this epic conflict", and that "the third and last contest took place in the closing pages of *The Hollow Needle*".[3] I am by no means sure that this sequence of events is necessarily right. An obvious parallel occurs in the

---

[1] As presumably did Ellery Queen. The book contains no internal evidence to suggest otherwise.
[2] My earliest copy is the American edition of 1910, published by J. S. Ogilvie under the title *The Extraordinary Adventures of Arsène Lupin, Gentleman Burglar*. "The Seven of Hearts" is one of the stories.   [3] *Op. cit.*, p. 14.

English canon of Sherlock Holmes cases. *The Hound of the Baskervilles* was published as a book in 1902, but the events described in it pre-date those recorded in "The Final Problem", contained in *The Memoirs of Sherlock Holmes* which had appeared as a single volume as early as 1894.

I agree with Ellery Queen that the last meeting between Holmes and Lupin took place in *The Hollow Needle*, for the internal evidence in that book seems to me to be conclusive on the point, as I hope to show. On the other hand, the evidence in regard to the chronology of their first encounter is conflicting, a state of affairs which is equally true of a number of matters which for many years have engaged the attention of textual critics of the Baker Street canon. A case can undoubtedly be made out that "the opening skirmish occurred" in *Arsène Lupin versus Holmlock Shears* and not, as Ellery Queen asserts, in "Holmlock Shears Arrives Too Late". It may clarify what follows if I remark that the meeting between Holmes and Lupin described in *Arsène Lupin versus Holmlock Shears* took place in a small restaurant near a Paris railway station. In "Holmlock Shears Arrives Too Late", it occurred on a country road.

I suggest, as a preliminary gambit, that the last word on the subject by Lupin's anonymous biographer must obviously be accepted as that contained in *The Hollow Needle*. On page 116 he described the first encounter between France's national gentleman-burglar and Isidore Beautrelet, the brilliant schoolboy-detective. He compared it with what he described flatly as Lupin's "first meeting" with Sherlock Holmes:

> "I had been present at the first meeting between Lupin and [Holmes] in the café near the Gare Montparnasse, and I could not help recalling the haughty carriage of the two combatants, the terrific clash of their pride under the politeness of their manners, the hard blows which they dealt each other, their feints, their arrogance. Here [in the case of Beautrelet] it was quite different."

The first fact to which I invite Ellery Queen's attention is that this account in *The Hollow Needle* of "the first meeting" is linked to a footnote at the bottom of the page (p. 116) "*Arsène Lupin versus Holmlock Shears*, by Maurice Leblanc", which, in isolation, would seem to demolish without further argument the assertion by Ellery Queen that "the opening skirmish occurred in 'Holmlock Shears Arrives Too Late' ". The second fact is that the literature contains only one account of a meeting between Holmes and Lupin in a café, and this indeed occurs on pp. 77–91 of *Arsène Lupin versus Holmlock Shears*, thus confirming the footnote in *The Hollow Needle*:

> "We were dining near the Gare du Nord, inside a little restaurant where Arsène Lupin had invited me to join him."

I must concede that Lupin's biographer's memory was slightly at fault in *The Hollow Needle* in regard to the actual railway station, but this seems to me to be of no consequence. These slips of the pen are common, even with the best of biographers. Dr. Watson's recording of Holmes's cases frequently confused months,[1] years,[2] and even Watson's own forename.[3]

Before the arrival of Holmes and Watson at the café, Lupin remarked to his biographer:

> "To begin with, there's the question of my vanity: they consider that I'm worth asking the famous Englishman to meet. Next, think of the pleasure which a fighter like myself must take in the prospect of a duel with [Sherlock Holmes]. Well, I shall have to exert myself to the utmost." (p. 81).

These words strongly suggest, it may be thought, that the first meeting and the first "duel" with Sherlock Holmes, whilst imminent, were still to come. Shortly afterwards, when Holmes and Watson had joined Lupin and his biographer in the café, a memorable conversation took place (over whiskies and sodas) which seemed entirely to justify the later reference to it in *The Hollow Needle*:

> "[Lupin] 'For me to be arrested there would have to be a conjunction of such unlikely circumstances, a series of such stupefying pieces of ill-luck, that I cannot admit the possibility'.

---

[1] Watson variously described the events in the Sholto case as having taken place in July and September, 1888. (*The Sign of Four*, *L*., pp. 155 and 160).

[2] Watson recorded in his notebook that the case of John Scott Eccles occurred on "a bleak and windy day towards the end of March in the year 1892". (*Wisteria Lodge*, *S*., p. 891.) Between May, 1891 (*The Final Problem*, *S*., p. 552), and the spring of 1894, however (*The Empty House*, *S*., p. 559), Watson was continuously mourning Holmes's death.

[3] John H. Watson, M.D., of *A Study in Scarlet* (*L*., p. vii), was later called "James" by his wife. (*The Man with the Twisted Lip*, *S*., p. 125.)

[Holmes] 'What neither circumstances nor luck may be able to effect, M. Lupin, can be brought about by one man's will and persistence'.

[Lupin] 'If the will and persistence of another man do not oppose an invincible obstacle to that plan, Mr. [Holmes]'.

[Holmes] 'There is no such thing as an invincible obstacle, M. Lupin'.

The two exchanged a penetrating glance, free from provocation on either side, but calm and fearless. It was the clash of two swords about to open the combat. It sounded clear and frank.

'Joy!' cried Lupin. 'Here's a man at last!'." (p. 90).

It will be seen that on the evidence just quoted from *Arsène Lupin versus Holmlock Shears*, and more especially the flat statement in retrospect in *The Hollow Needle* that the first meeting between Holmes and Lupin had taken place in a café near a Paris railway station, the matter must be regarded as beyond dispute and Ellery Queen cannot be other than mistaken. Unfortunately for me, however, a remark by Lupin to his biographer in the restuarant, before the actual encounter with Holmes, is recorded on p. 82 of *Arsène Lupin versus Holmlock Shears*, accompanied by a footnote just as damning to my case as the one I have quoted from *The Hollow Needle* against Ellery Queen:-

" 'He will recognize me,' said Arsène Lupin. 'He saw me only once,[1] but I felt that he saw me for life and that what he saw was not my appearance, which I can always alter, but the very being that I am'."

The footnote at the bottom of p. 82, to which the superior "1" refers is just as conclusive in its content as mine from *The Hollow Needle*, which it flatly contradicts:-

"[1] See *The Seven of Hearts*, by Maurice Leblanc. Chapter IX: 'Holmlock Shears Arrives Too Late'."

It may well be that it is upon this passage and this footnote that Ellery Queen rests his assertion that the first encounter unquestionably took place in "Holmlock Shears Arrives Too Late", although he does not say so, and does not quote the evidence that contradicts it.

It may be thought that at this point, Ellery Queen and I

confront each other as textual critics of equivalent stature, or, more picturesquely, as an irresistible force and an immovable object, like Holmes and Lupin who, in Ellery Queen's words, "never achieved more than a draw". I suggest that in these circumstances the matter can only be resolved by a further examination of the themes and the texts of "Holmlock Shears Arrives Too Late" and *Arsène Lupin versus Holmlock Shears*. Only additional evidence will settle the matter of precedence once and for all.

"Holmlock Shears Arrives Too Late" is concerned with the robbery by Lupin of some of the art treasures of Thibermesnil Castle in Normandy, which included "six Louis XV armchairs and as many occasional chairs, a number of Aubusson tapestries, some candelabra signed by Gouthière, two Fragonards and a Nattier, a bust by Houdon, and . . . a unique collection of watches, snuffboxes, rings, chatelaines, miniatures of the most exquisite workmanship" (p. 22)[1]. Holmes was invited by the owner, Georges Devanne, not only to solve the mystery of the theft, but also the related historical puzzle of a supposed secret entry to the castle, to which enigmatic clues were contained in a sixteenth-century book of exceptional rarity, *The Chronicles of Thibermesnil*. It seems probable that Holmes's early success in deciphering *The Musgrave Ritual*, "the strange catechism to which each Musgrave had to submit when he came to man's estate"[2] had been an ingredient in the reason for Devanne incurring the presumably enormous expense of persuading the great detective to come to France. The secret of Thibermesnil Castle, "that the high and mighty lords handed down to one another, on their death-beds, from father to son" (p. 18) had obvious similarities to the ancient riddle of the manor house at Hurlstone in Sussex.

In the Devanne affair, the problem was accentuated by the concurrent, inexplicable disappearance of the only two known copies of *The Chronicles of Thibermesnil*, from the Castle library and the Bibliothèque Nationale. But Holmes was, as Devanne pointed out, "the great English detective, for whom no mystery

[1] The page references are to "Holmlock Shears Arrives Too Late" in *The Misadventures of Sherlock Holmes*.
[2] *The Musgrave Ritual*, S., p. 407.

exists, the most extraordinary solver of riddles that has ever been known, the wonderful individual who might have been the creation of a novelist's brain". (p. 17). Holmes quickly solved the historical puzzle of Thibermesnil and found the secret passage from the castle to the ruined chapel in the park, and the subsequent conversation between the astonished Devanne and Holmes was truly Baker Street in its flavour:

> " 'It's wonderful, marvellous, and just as simple as ABC! How is it that the mystery was never seen through?'
>
> 'Because nobody ever united the three or four necessary elements; that is to say, the two books and the quotations . . . nobody, except Arsène Lupin and myself'.
>
> 'But I also', said Devanne, 'and the Abbe Gelis . . . we both of us knew as much about it as you, and yet . . ., [Holmes] smiled.
>
> 'Monsieur Devanne, it is not given to all the world to succeed in solving riddles'.
>
> 'But I have been hunting for ten years. And you, in ten minutes . . .'
>
> 'Pooh! It's a matter of habit'." (p. 36)

It is fair to recall, however, that it was Lupin himself who quixotically returned the art treasures to Thibermesnil (in the care of a quartermaster sergeant, in two military wagons) because of his love for Nellie Underwood.

Earlier in the story Lupin, disguised as the artist Horace Velmont,[1] was on his way from Thibermesnil to the railway station. As he expected, he encountered Holmes, who Lupin knew was on his way to the castle for his first meeting with his client Devanne. Holmes asked for directions to Thibermesnil which Lupin courteously provided. Brief pleasantries as between strangers were exchanged. Despite both Ellery Queen's belief that this meeting was "the opening skirmish", and such of the evidence that superficially supports such a view, it seems to me that two quoted unspoken thoughts of Lupin are solidly against such a conclusion. He said to Holmes that he was one of the great detective's most fervent admirers, and immediately regretted "the slightest shade of irony in his voice", for Holmes looked at him so keenly that despite his disguise Lupin was constrained to wonder, "Did he recognize me or not?"

[1] We meet Horace Velmont again in "The Wedding-Ring" in the rare *The Confessions of Arsène Lupin* (London, 1912).

As the two men exchanged bows, "a noise of hoofs rang out, the clinking sound of horses trotting along the road. It was the gendarmes". Because the road was narrow, Holmes and Lupin had to draw to one side together, in the grass, to allow the cavalcade to go by.

> "The gendarmes passed, and as they were riding in single file, at quite a distance each from the other, this took some time. Lupin thought:
>
> 'It all depends upon whether he recognised me. If so, does he intend to take his advantage?'
>
> When the last horseman had passed, [Sherlock Holmes] drew himself up and without saying a word, brushed the dust from his clothes." (p. 30)

Lupin's unspoken anxiety, twice quoted, as to whether Holmes's powers of observation had pierced his disguise as Horace Velmont and recognized him as Arsène Lupin, is inexplicable if this was indeed their first meeting.

It is also relevant to consider dates. In "Holmlock Shears Arrives Too Late" the great detective was described as a man of middle age, clean-shaven and thin-lipped, with extraordinarily piercing eyes. The mention of his age is not precise, but the word picture suggests that he was over fifty. Accepted experts in the biography of Sherlock Holmes such as Gavin Brend,[1] W. S. Baring-Gould,[2] Sir Sydney Roberts,[3] H. W. Bell[4] and E. B. Zeisler[5] have respectively (and variously) placed Holmes's year of birth as 1853, 1854, 1854, late 1854 or 1855, and 1857 or 1858. Whatever date we adopt (even 1852, favoured by Mr. T. S. Blakeney, Holmes's first biographer, and myself) it seems clear that this visit to France must unquestionably have taken place after Holmes's retirement from Baker Street in 1903[6] to his villa on the edge of the South Downs "commanding a great view of the Channel", where "the coast-line is entirely of chalk cliffs".[7] In this connexion it is perhaps of some significance that the place of Holmes's departure from France at the conclusion of the Devanne case

[1] *My Dear Holmes* (London, 1951), p. 16.   [2] *op. cit.* p. 11.
[3] *Holmes & Watson. A Miscellany* (London, 1953), p. 17.   [4] *op. cit.* p. 4.
[5] *Baker Street Chronology* (Chicago, 1953), p. 141.
[6] *The Creeping Man, S.,* p. 1244.
[7] *The Lion's Mane, S.,* p. 1267.

was conveniently chosen by him. He sailed from Dieppe, we are told, and therefore disembarked at Newhaven in Sussex, only a few miles from Cuckmere Haven, the Seven Sisters and the other features of this beautiful coast, so closely associated with Sherlock Holmes during his later years of comparative leisure.

The fact that Watson did not accompany Holmes to Thibermesnil may also be regarded as suggestive in its support of the idea that the events in "Holmlock Shears Arrives Too Late" took place during the post-Baker Street years on the South Downs, of which Holmes wrote:

> "At this period of my life the good Watson had passed almost beyond my ken. An occasional week-end visit was the most that I ever saw of him. Thus I must act as my own chronicler."[1]

In striking contrast with the Watson-less "Holmlock Shears Arrives Too Late", "Dr. Wilson" was very much in evidence in *Arsène Lupin versus Holmlock Shears* (p. 204).[2] At this period the two friends were still sharing the famous sitting-room at "219 Parker Street" in London (p. 76) occupying their familiar easy-chairs on either side of the fireplace:

> "The great detective's pipe had gone out. He knocked the ashes into the grate, refilled his briar, lit it, [and] gathered the skirts of his dressing-gown around his knees." (p. 201).

In parenthesis, it is in this record that the identification of Holmes by his French chronicler, under what must be the thinnest ever of all pseudonyms, is most marked. Lupin said of him, "As a detective, I doubt if his equal exists, or has ever existed" (p. 81). Leblanc left the matter in no doubt when he wrote:

> "And then, of course, he is Holmlock Shears, that is to say, a sort of miracle of intuition, of insight, of perspicacity, of shrewdness. It is as though Nature had amused herself by taking the two most extraordinary types of detective that fiction had invented, Poe's Dupin and Garboriau's Lecoq, in order to build up one in her own fashion, more extraordinary yet and more unreal. And, upon my word, any one hearing of the adventures which have made the name

[1] *The Lion's Mane, S.,* p. 1266.
[2] The page references are to the second edition of 1911.

64

of Holmlock Shears famous all over the world must feel inclined to ask if he is not a legendary person, a hero who has stepped straight from the brain of some great novel-writer, of a Conan Doyle, for instance." (p. 85).

"Shears" was, of course, "the famous Englishman" (p. 81). The Countess de Crozon's awed reference to him, "There is one man and one man only", (p. 75) is surely a precise French parallel of an opinion of German provenance:

> "Von Bork sat up in amazement. 'There is only one man,' he cried."[1]

Just as the pre-occupations of Holmes's enormous consulting practice made it difficult for him to leave London when, for example, "one of the most revered names in England is being besmirched by a blackmailer",[2] so a similar problem arose in *Arsène Lupin versus Holmlock Shears:*

> "I am very busy. There's the robbery at the Anglo-Chinese Bank; and Lady Eccleston has been kidnapped, as you know." (p. 85).

One of Holmes's typical fits of "lethargy, during which he would lie about with his violin and his books, hardly moving", alternating with "outbursts of passionate energy"[3] was in evidence in *Arsène Lupin versus Holmlock Shears*, when, after spending a whole afternoon doing nothing but smoke and doze, he announced to his biographer that he was at last ready to resume the investigation (p. 109). It is almost superfluous to say that throughout the whole case the detective was constantly smoking, refilling and relighting his pipe (pp. 87, 93, etc.). The comparison of Holmes with a foxhound "as, with gleaming eyes and straining muscles, it runs upon a breast-high scent"[4] in London was supplemented in Paris in *Arsène Lupin versus Holmlock Shears* when the great detective "sniffed the air greedily, like a good hound scenting a fresh trail" (p. 124). Demonstrations by Holmes of his skill in the art of the conjurer in *A Study in Scarlet*, *The Mazarin Stone* and *The Naval Treaty*[5]

---

[1] *His Last Bow*, S., p. 1084.
[2] *The Hound of the Baskervilles*, L., p. 321.
[3] *The Musgrave Ritual*, S., p. 397.
[4] *The Bruce-Partington Plans*, S., p. 980.
[5] This facet of the detective's personality is discussed on pp. 102–3 of Hall, I.

are recalled by the sleight-of-hand with the captain's watch by the great English detective on board the yacht *Hirondelle*. Even Lupin was constrained to compliment the Englishman, "Well done, well done! It's a good trick and I must remember it". (p. 181). That Holmes possessed "a great heart as well as a great brain" was shown when Watson was shot in the thigh by Killer Evans:

> "You're not hurt, Watson? For God's sake, say that you are not hurt!"[1]

These admirable sentiments were repeated by the detective when "Dr. Wilson" was stabbed, in *Arsène Lupin versus Holmlock Shears:*

> "Wilson, Wilson, it's not serious, is it? Say it's only a scratch!" (p. 221)

In the Lupin adventures involving Sherlock Holmes none of the incidents, nor any of the newspapers and letters quoted in the text, are dated, either purposefully or by implication, with one imprecise exception, which occurs on p. 172 of *Arsène Lupin versus Holmlock Shears*. A house in Paris which had been used by Lupin and his associates had been discovered by Holmes, as a result of some remarkable deductions by him in regard to the work of a distinguished architect, Lucien Destange. Lupin was forced to leave, but before doing so he drew a large chalk circle on the dark wall-paper of the dining-room and wrote in it, after the style of a commemorative tablet:

> "Arsène Lupin, Gentleman Burglar, lived here for 5 years at the commencement of the twentieth century."

This phrasing is not easy to interpret with precision. Clearly Lupin was there for five years, but what does "at the commencement of the twentieth century" mean? Did Lupin actually live in the house from 1901 to 1905, and was 1905 therefore the year of the events described in *Arsène Lupin versus Holmlock Shears*? If this was so, then it would be flatly contradicted by all the other evidence, and in particular by the facts that Holmes and Watson were still living together in London and that the

---

[1] *The Three Garridebs*, S., p. 1213.

detective was still in active practice, investigating simultaneously the Crozon affair and those of the Anglo-Chinese Bank and Lady Eccleston. We know that the matter of Professor Presbury of Camford, which Holmes cleared up in September, 1903, "was one of the very last cases handled by Holmes before his retirement from practice",[1] so clearly 1905 is an impossible year for the events occurring in *Arsène Lupin versus Holmlock Shears*.

At this period Holmes was "about fifty years of age" distinguished by his "keen, bright, penetrating eyes" (pp. 84–5). If Holmes's year of birth was 1852, as both Mr. T. S. Blakeney and I have calculated,[2] this would place the French case in 1902 or thereabouts, which would be perfectly possible. Lupin's occupation of the Paris house would therefore be from 1898 to 1902, to which the expression "5 years at the commencement of the twentieth century" is not inapplicable. It is of additional interest to notice in this connexion that a biographical dictionary consulted by Holmes showed that Lucien Destange, Grand-Prix de Rome, Officer of the Legion of Honour and author of several valuable works on architecture, was born in 1840 (p. 115). At the time of *Arsène Lupin versus Holmlock Shears* Destange had retired from practice and was living in a "magnificent house at the corner of the Place Malesherbes and the Rue Montchanin", where Holmes was received by the butler (p. 118). The famous architect, who was an enthusiastic book-collector, had entirely relinquished his professional work to devote the whole of his time to his enormous library of old and rare books on architecture, a collection contained in "a large circular room, which occupied one of the wings of the house and which was lined with books all round the walls". (p. 119). The library was so large and valuable that Destange had decided that it would be desirable to prepare a general catalogue of his collection "and of the German books in particular" (p. 119). At the time of *Arsène Lupin versus Holmlock Shears*, he was busily engaged on this task with secretarial assistance.

A magnificent house in a fashionable part of Paris, a butler, a private secretary and a large library of rare and valuable

---

[1] *The Creeping Man, S.*, p. 1244.
[2] Blakeney, *op. cit.*, p. 3, and Hall, I, p. 77.

books, all point unmistakably to the fact that Destange was a man of very considerable wealth, which was entirely to be expected at the end of a professional life so distinguished and successful that he had received two coveted decorations and was listed in the French equivalent of *Who's Who*. It can scarcely be doubted that such a man, eager to devote his whole time to his hobby and possessed of a large fortune, would retire from professional life at the age of sixty at the latest, that is to say in 1900. We may think that the preparation of the catalogue of his great library was a congenial task to which Destange had long looked forward, and to which he would begin to devote himself as soon as retirement was possible. Since he was still engaged upon it when Holmes and he met, a year of 1901 or 1902 is again strongly suggested and is entirely appropriate.

I have said earlier in this essay that I agree with Ellery Queen that *The Hollow Needle* is undoubtedly the last of the sequence. Holmes[1] played a less important role than usual in this mystery, mainly set in Normandy, and the fascinating riddle of the Étretat Needle and the historic false trail to the Château de l'Aiguille in the Department of the Creuse was actually solved by Isidore Beautrelet, a sixth-form pupil at the Lycée Janson-de-Sailly in Paris. One of the clues to which Beautrelet properly attached great importance was the significant fact that like all the historical events connected with the mystery of the Hollow Needle, many of Lupin's previous exploits had also occurred in that part of Normandy bounded by Rouen, Dieppe and Le Havre. Any argument is settled by the fact that of the seven geographically significant incidents of this kind recalled and listed by Beautrelet (p. 224), one had been recorded in *Arsène Lupin versus Holmlock Shears* and the remainder in *The Exploits of Arsène Lupin*, the collection of stories, it will be remembered, that had included "Holmlock Shears Arrives Too Late".

So there it is. On what seems to me to be the overwhelming weight of the evidence, despite one admitted contradictory feature, I place the chronological sequence of the events of the duel between Sherlock Holmes and Arsène Lupin, as recorded

[1] As we would expect in a case which, like that of "Holmlock Shears Arrives Too Late", occurred after Holmes's retirement to Sussex, Watson is not in evidence in *The Hollow Needle*.

by Maurice Leblanc, firmly as *Arsène Lupin versus Holmlock Shears*, "Holmlock Shears Arrives Too Late" and *The Hollow Needle*. I hope that Ellery Queen will allow me to add "Q.E.D." by a graceful capitulation.

VII

THE ORIGIN OF SHERLOCK HOLMES

O N the front cover of *Ellery Queen's Mystery Magazine* of February, 1971,[1] was the announcement "EXTRA-SPECIAL. The most important Sherlockian discovery in 40 years! MICHAEL HARRISON reveals the true origin of Sherlock Holmes." The essay, "A Study in Surmise", by the distinguished author of *In the Footsteps of Sherlock Holmes* (London, 1958), was hailed as of first importance and interest to all students of the Baker Street canon by Ellery Queen, Vincent Starrett, Howard Haycraft, Rex Stout and Dr. Julian Wolff. I am indebted to Ellery Queen for drawing my attention to this essay, and for kindly presenting me with a copy of his magazine containing it.

What Mr. Harrison has set out to prove is that Conan Doyle was inspired to write *A Study in Scarlet* wholly by the curious case of the disappearance in London of a German baker, Urban Napoleon Stanger, on 12 November, 1881. Stanger's bakery was at 136 Lever Street, St. Luke's, in the East End of London, and when the affair received wide press publicity following the arrest of Franz Felix Stumm on 12 September, 1882, on a charge of forgery, it became universally known as "The St. Luke's Mystery". Stumm, who was also of German birth, was Stanger's manager and the lover of his employer's wife, Elizabeth Stanger. Stumm was tried at the Old Bailey and found guilty by the jury. He was sentenced to ten years penal servitude by Mr. Justice Hawkins.

The sequence of events from Stanger's disappearance in 1881 to the arrest of Stumm in 1882 can only be epitomised here.

---

[1] Henceforward referred to as *EQMM*.

Both Stumm and Mrs. Stanger told enquirers that Stanger had returned to Germany, and that he was living in Kreuznach, Hesse-Cassel, although subsequent investigation in that town by Inspector Henry Radike of Scotland Yard failed to discover any trace there of the missing baker. In January, 1882, after this story was first put about by Stumm and Mrs. Stanger, an anxious friend of Stanger's, George Geisel, was regaled with an entirely different account by Stumm. Geisel was told that Stanger was recuperating in the country, "having broken a blood vessel".[1] To confuse matters further, a few days later Geisel received a letter purporting to come from Stanger in Germany, which was so clumsy a forgery that he was not even momentarily deceived.

These palpable evasions caused Geisel to become suspicious and profoundly disturbed about the disappearance of his friend, and he employed a private inquiry agent, a fellow-German named Wendel Scherer in business in London, to investigate the circumstances of the vanishing of Urban Stanger, and authorised him to offer a reward of £50 for any information that might lead to the discovery of the missing baker. Scherer's inquiries were unsuccessful, the reward was never claimed, and after a few frustrating weeks Geisel reported the matter to the police with the ultimate result already mentioned. Whatever suspicions there may have been in regard to other possible crimes by Stumm, actual proof was only available for his having forged a cheque on Stanger's bank account, an offence of which he was found guilty and suffered a severe prison sentence.

Forgery has always been an indictable offence, and Stumm was initially committed for trial at Worship Street Police Court by Henry Jeffreys Busby, a London magistrate. Wendel Scherer, the inquiry agent, gave evidence at the committal proceedings, and was severely criticised by the magistrate for his airs and graces in claiming to be "a private consulting detective". The magistrate considered that for Scherer to regard himself as a "professional gentleman" was preposterous, and the following reported exchange exemplifies the scorn with which Mr. Busby evidently regarded the status of a late nineteenth-century inquiry agent in London:

[1] *EQMM,* p. 63.

"SCHERER: I am a professional gentleman; I am a professional consulting detective. This is why I must respectfully preserve the anonymity of my client [Geisel]. It would be a grave breach of professional etiquette were I to reveal his name.

MR. BUSBY: Hoity-toity, sir, you try my patience a little too far! I should commit you for contempt! An inquiry agent, of which half a dozen advertise their services every day in the newspapers—and we have these preposterous claims of yours to professional dignity, professional secrecy, and I don't know what else! Stand down, sir; but do not leave the Court—I shall wish to speak with you later!"[1]

Whatever we may think of this outburst by the infuriated magistrate, it must be conceded that Scherer's position was weakened by the fact that he had failed to solve the case.

Mr. Harrison tells us that "there was one avid reader of the newspapers [in 1882] who disagreed with the Magistrate and felt a warm sympathy with the detective. This was Dr. Conan Doyle."[2] Mr. Harrison supports this assertion, admittedly speculative, by reminding us that in later life Doyle was to display a similar instinctive sympathy toward George Edalji and Oscar Slater, both of whom he considered had been wrongly condemned, and suggests that it would be entirely natural for the young author's thoughts to move on from poor Scherer in a direction that inevitably caused Doyle to decide to write *A Study in Scarlet*:

"But suppose such a man *justifiably* called himself a private consulting detective?—a man with as tender a regard for his professional status as ever Mr. Wendel Scherer claimed, but with professional *efficiency*, professional *integrity*, true, unchallenged professional *standing*, to back up his self-esteem? . . . What would happen if a *real* private consulting detective had been pitted, in a mystery such as St. Luke's, against the professionals of Scotland Yard?."[3]

And so, writes Mr. Harrison, Wendel Scherer was "the real-life person in whom Sherlock Holmes originated".[4] He tells us that if Holmes is not exactly Wendel Scherer, then Holmes is Scherer as he might and ought to have been. Holmes, he says, is Scherer idealized. These are large claims, and we would be

[1] *EQMM*, p. 66.   [2] *EQMM*, p. 67.   [3] *EQMM*, p. 67.
[4] *EQMM*. p. 74.

right to regard them as purely speculative if Mr. Harrison did not offer some evidence to support them. The consideration of that evidence resolves itself into a simple question. Is there sufficient indication in the text of *A Study in Scarlet* to make it seem certain that Doyle's choice of names, dates, places and other circumstances in his first Sherlock Holmes story was dictated by a deep study of the St. Luke's Mystery? Mr. Harrison goes even further than this when he says that Doyle purposefully inserted clues to the Stanger affair in *A Study in Scarlet*:

> "Doyle did not wish the reader to forget that his story owed its inspiration to The St. Luke's Mystery, so, as I shall now prove, the real-life case is echoed again and again in Conan Doyle's *A Study in Scarlet*."[1]

I think that Mr. Harrison would concede that some of the points of supposed resemblance between the case and the story listed by him would not merit serious consideration by themselves. Mr. Harrison's assertion in juxtaposition with his note "Stumm charged with forgery of cheque for £76. 15s.",[2] for example, is that the "loose money to the extent of seven pounds thirteen" found in the pockets of the murdered Enoch J. Drebber[3] was "a sum *exactly one-tenth* of that mentioned in Stumm's indictment".[4] Mr. Harrison's italics are persuasive, but his arithmetic is incorrect. It follows that his elaboration of this mathematical theme, his suggestion that the presence in Drebber's pocket of a copy of Boccaccio's *Decameron*, "a book with the element 'ten' (Greek, *deka* = ten) in the title"[5] was another deeply subtle clue inserted by Doyle, must also fall to pieces in its turn. It may be thought, too, that because the famous Eagle Tavern in City Road was not far from Stanger's bakery in Lever Street, we need not necessarily jump to the conclusion, as Mr. Harrison does, that this must have been Doyle's inspiration for the place-name "Eagle Cañon" in the Mormon section of *A Study in Scarlet*.[6] "Doyle gives Drebber the Christian name of the Prophet Enoch, memorable for having disappeared", writes Mr. Harrison, who sees a significant

---

[1] *EQMM*, p. 70. [2] *EQMM*, p. 70 [3] *A Study in Scarlet*, L., p. 33.
[4] *EQMM*, p. 70. [5] *EQMM*, p. 70.
[6] *EQMM*, p. 72 and *A Study in Scarlet*, L., p. 108

connexion between this and the disappearance of Stanger.[1] These and similar ideas are ingenious, but the evidence is surely too tenuous, we may think, for them to be used, as Mr. Harrison does use them, to support his introductory assertion: "As I shall now *prove* [my italics], the real-life case is echoed again and again in Conan Doyle's *A Study in Scarlet*."[2]

On the other hand, it must be conceded that the similarity between the names of Enoch J. Drebber's secretary, Joseph Stangerson, of *A Study in Scarlet* and Urban Napoleon Stanger of the "St. Luke's Mystery" is curious, and Mr. Harrison is justified in calling our attention to it.[3] The real-life case had a solid German background, as Mr. Harrison points out, and it is also therefore admittedly odd to find a faint German flavour (entirely false though it proved to be) emanating from a solitary incident in *A Study in Scarlet*. Mr. Harrison draws our attention to the fact that Jefferson Hope "after his nose has bled over the dead Drebber, dips his finger in the blood and writes the German word *Rache* (revenge) on the wall of the empty room".[4] It is a considerable over-statement, however, for Mr. Harrison to assert, as he does, that this is proof of a "strong German element retained in *A Study in Scarlet*, despite the superficial 'Americanization' ".[5] It is nothing of the kind, and to demolish it we have merely to consult the text of *A Study in Scarlet*. Of the word "Rache" Holmes said to Watson:

> "As to poor Lestrade's discovery, it was simply a blind intended to put the police upon a wrong track, by suggesting Socialism and secret societies. It was not done by a German. The A, if you noticed, was printed somewhat after the German fashion. Now, a real German invariably prints in the Latin character, so that we may safely say that this was not written by one, but by a clumsy imitator who overdid his part. It was simply a ruse to divert inquiry into a wrong channel."[6]

Holmes's conclusion was proved to be completely accurate when Jefferson Hope made a clean breast of the matter:

> "I remembered a German being found [dead] in New York with RACHE written up above him, and it was argued at the time in the

[1] *EQMM*, p. 71.   [2] *EQMM*, p. 70.   [3] *EQMM*, p. 70.
[4] *EQMM*, p. 72.   [5] *EQMM*, p. 70.
[6] *A Study in Scarlet*, L., p. 39.

newspapers that the secret societies must have done it. I guessed that what puzzled the New Yorkers would puzzle the Londoners, so I dipped my finger in my own blood and printed it on a convenient place on the wall."[1]

Mr. Harrison's "strong German element" in *A Study in Scarlet* is thus reduced to a simple mystification, entirely bogus in its origin. As to the alleged "superficial" nature of the American aspect of the case, the roots of *A Study in Scarlet* were in fact solidly embedded in the United States. The murderer Jefferson Hope and his two victims Enoch J. Drebber and Joseph Stangerson, were all Americans. The killings took place in London simply because Drebber and Stangerson had fled from Cleveland, Ohio when they knew that Hope had traced them there, and thence to St. Petersburg, Paris, Copenhagen and finally to the English capital, where Hope "at last succeeded in running them to earth".[2] The action of five chapters of *A Study in Scarlet* takes place in America, and the whole basis of the mystery originated in the New World.

Mr. Harrison makes further play with Jefferson Hope's bleeding nose by reminding us that one of the stories put about by Stumm to explain the disappearance of Stanger was that the latter was recuperating in the country from the effects of a broken blood vessel.[3] I agree that these less tenuous resemblances between the St. Luke's case and *A Study in Scarlet* do suggest that Doyle, in common with most readers of newspapers in 1882, had been interested in the details of the Stanger affair and had not forgotten them. What I do beg leave to doubt, however, is that the unsuccessful German private inquiry agent, Wendel Scherer, was "the true origin of Sherlock Holmes". I cannot agree with Mr. Harrison when he writes:

> "The fictional detective who was emerging into vigorous, highly individual life in Conan Doyle's brain was intended, by his creator, to be all the fine things that the real-life Wendel Scherer was—as well as many things that Scherer was not . . . While the Stanger-Stumm-Scherer case was still fresh in his memory, Dr. Conan Doyle, in one of those long waits between patients, smoothed out a leaf in his notebook and began to make some notes."[4]

[1] *A Study in Scarlet*, L., pp. 130–1. [2] *Ibid.*, L. p. 120.
[3] *EQMM*, p. 70. [4] *EQMM*, p. 69.

The principal weakness in this argument is that it is not supported by the relevant dates and facts in Doyle's life. The newspaper accounts of the St. Luke's Mystery appeared in 1882. Doyle did not begin to write *A Study in Scarlet* until March, 1886,[1] and during those four intervening years Doyle's literary output was considerable, but none of it indicated any immediate interest in the writing of a detective story. If the inspiration and "the true origin of Sherlock Holmes" was the trial of Wendel Scherer in 1882, then it may be thought that the period of gestation was oddly protracted. If Doyle's enthusiasm to write *A Study in Scarlet* described by Mr. Harrison owed everything to the Stanger affair, then it is hard to understand Doyle's omission to include the smallest reference to it in his autobiography or anywhere else. His own account of the birth of *A Study in Scarlet* differed completely from that suggested by Mr. Harrison:

"It was about a year after my marriage[2] that I realized that I could go on writing short stories for ever[3] and never make headway. What is necessary is that your name should be on the back of a volume. Only so do you assert your individuality, and get the full credit or discredit for your achievement. I had for some time from 1884 onwards been engaged upon a sensational book of adventure which I had called 'The Firm of Girdlestone', which represented my first attempt at a connected narrative . . . I felt now that I was capable of something fresher and crisper and more workmanlike. Gaboriau had rather attracted me by the neat dovetailing of his plots, and Poe's masterful detective, M. Dupin, had from boyhood been one of my heroes. But could I bring an addition of my own? I thought of my old teacher Joe Bell, of his eagle face, of his curious ways, of his eerie trick of spotting details. If he were a detective he would surely reduce this fascinating but unorganized business to something nearer to an exact science. I would try if I could get this effect . . . The idea amused me. What should I call the fellow? I still possess the leaf of a notebook with various alternative names."[4]

[1] Carr, p. 65.

[2] Doyle married his first wife, Louise Hawkins, on 6 August, 1885.

[3] Between 1882, the year of the press reports of the St. Luke's Mystery, and 1886 Doyle contributed numerous stories and articles to *London Society*, *Good Words*, *The Boy's Own Paper*, *Cornhill*, *Cassell's* and *Blackwoods'*, in addition to writing *The Firm of Girdlestone*, which was ultimately published in 1890 (Harold Locke, *A Bibliographical Catalogue of the Writings of Sir Arthur Conan Doyle*, Tunbridge Wells, 1928, and Nordon, pp. 347–50, "Bibliography").

[4] *Memories*, pp. 74–5.

Doyle was referring in the last two sentences to the now famous page of his Southsea notebook on which he wrote down the first conception of *A Study in Scarlet* and the experimental and final names of Holmes and Watson. "And so I had my puppets and wrote my *Study in Scarlet*", he told us.[1] The page was headed "A Study in Scarlet", and was preserved by the author and later by Adrian Conan Doyle. It has been photographically reproduced in many books about Doyle and Sherlock Holmes.[2] It duly appears on page 68 of Mr. Harrison's essay, and it is to this historical document that he is referring when he tells us on the opposite page 69 that while the Stanger-Stumm-Scherer case was still fresh in Doyle's mind in 1882, the creator of Sherlock Holmes "smoothed out a page of his notebook and began to make some notes. What he wrote is shown, in holograph, on the facing page." It will not do, for we know from Doyle himself that the page was written in 1886, "about a year after my marriage" in 1885.

Doyle's reference to "my old teacher, Joseph Bell", of whom he thought when he was constructing the personality and abilities of Sherlock Holmes, is given rather short shrift by Mr. Harrison. He concedes that Dr. Joseph Bell of Edinburgh is "officially" (the quotation marks are his) said to be the original of Sherlock Holmes,[3] and that Holmes's "snap deductions" were clearly based on similar demonstrations by Bell, but concludes:

> "In this one respect—a most important respect, of course—Holmes owes something of his origin to Dr. Joseph Bell; in every other respect, including the points of name,[4] arrogance, pride, aggressiveness, and relative youth, he originates in the proud, principled—even if unsuccessful—private consulting detective, Mr. Wendel Scherer, of 28 Chepstow Place, Westbourne Grove."[5]

Despite Mr. Harrison's opinion, a formidable case can undoubtedly be made out that Joseph Bell was the model upon

---

[1] *Memories*, p. 75.

[2] See, for example, Starrett, *op. cit.*, p. 9, Nordon, p. 212, M. & M. Hardwick, *The Man Who Was Sherlock Holmes* (London, 1964), p. 33 and W. S. Baring-Gould, *The Annotated Sherlock Holmes* (London, 1968), i, p. 11.

[3] *EQMM*, p. 78.

[4] Mr. Harrison believes that Scherer's Christian name reminded Doyle of Oliver Wendell Holmes, and that the surname of the great detective was thus chosen (*EQMM*, p. 75).   [5] *EQMM*, p. 79.

which the character of the great detective was based, and if we are really to ascertain "the true origin of Sherlock Holmes", then Bell is certainly worthy of discussion. Dr. John Lamond, the first of Doyle's seven biographers, wrote with the brevity of conviction that "Dr. Joseph Bell, as is well known, became the prototype of Sherlock Holmes".[1] Lamond's immediate successor, Hesketh Pearson, said with firmness that Doyle had modelled Holmes on Dr. Bell,[2] and had portrayed "Dr. Bell (Sherlock Holmes)" at length in his books.[3] Let us see how far the facts support these assertions.

On the verso of the title-page of *The Adventures of Sherlock Holmes* (London, 1892) is printed the dedication, "To my old teacher Joseph Bell, M.D., &c. of 2, Melville Crescent, Edinburgh." In a letter to Dr. Bell of 4 May, 1892, Dr. Arthur Conan Doyle (as he was then) wrote:

> "It is most certainly to you that I owe Sherlock Holmes, and though in the stories I have the advantage of being able to place [the detective] in all sorts of dramatic positions, I do not think that his analytical work is in the least an exaggeration of some effects which I have seen you produce in the out-patient ward. Round the centre of deduction and inference and observation which I have heard you inculcate, I have tried to build up a man who pushed the thing as far as it would go—further occasionally—and I am so glad that the result satisfied you, who are the critic with the most right to be severe."

Opposite p. 48 of Howard Haycraft's *Murder for Pleasure. The Life and Times of the Detective Story* (London, 1942) is a plate with the overall legend, "They brought Sherlock Holmes into the World". Below are two head-and-shoulder photographs of "Dr. A. Conan Doyle as he looked in his Southsea years" and "Dr. Joseph Bell, of Edinburgh, on whom Conan Doyle founded the character".

Joseph Bell, M.D., F.R.C.S. (1837–1911), Consulting Surgeon to Edinburgh Royal Infirmary and the Royal Hospital for Sick Children, was 39 years old[4] when Doyle entered Edinburgh University in 1876 to read for the degree of Bachelor of Medicine. Bell was already the Editor of the

[1] Lamond, p. 7. [2] Pearson, p. 77. [3] Pearson, p. 12.
[4] And not in his "early forties", as suggested by Carr, p. 35.

Edinburgh Medical Journal, an appointment which he held from 1873 to 1896, and he was later to become a member of the Court of Edinburgh University, Deputy Lieutenant of Edinburgh and a Justice of the Peace for Midlothian. Doyle studied under Bell, and said of him in his autobiography that "his strong point was diagnosis, not only of disease, but of occupation and character". Doyle became Bell's "out-patient clerk", which meant that in the waiting room he made simple notes of each case before showing the patients, one by one, into the big room where Bell sat in state, surrounded by his dressers and students.

"He would sit in his receiving room", wrote Doyle, "with a face like a Red Indian, and diagnose the people as they came in, before they even opened their mouths. He would tell them their symptoms, and even give them details of their past life; and hardly ever would he make a mistake."

The results were often dramatic, as in the following dialogue between Bell and a civilian patient, recorded by Doyle in his autobiography:

> " 'Well, my man, you've served in the army.'
> 'Aye, sir.'
> 'Not long discharged?'
> 'No, sir.'
> 'A Highland regiment?'
> 'Aye, sir.'
> 'A non-com. officer?'
> 'Aye, sir.'
> 'Stationed at Barbados?'
> 'Aye, sir.'

'You see, gentlemen,' he would explain, 'the man was a respectful man but did not remove his hat. They do not in the army, but he would have learned civilian ways had he been long discharged. He has an air of authority and he is obviously Scottish. As to Barbados, his complaint is elephantiasis, which is West Indian and not British.' To his audience of Watsons it all seemed very miraculous until it was explained, and then it became simple enough. It is no wonder that after the study of such a character I used and amplified his methods when in later life I tried to build up a scientific detective who solved cases on his own merits and not through the folly of the criminal."[1]

[1] *Memories,* p. 26.

The Barbados dialogue was the only example of Bell's skill in observation and deduction recorded by Doyle in his memoirs. It was presumably this circumstance that caused Professor Nordon (apparently lacking knowledge of other comparable accounts of Bell that were not unavailable) to assert:

"This sketch of Joseph Bell takes us straight back to Sherlock Holmes. It is too like Holmes to be true. Conan Doyle never describes Bell in a way that allows us to distinguish him from his fictitious character; it is as if Bell only existed for him as the function of a literary illusion."[1]

Nordon suggests that Doyle's portrait of Bell was probably "not entirely accurate" and may indeed have been "an artifice", because it tells us little about Bell's mental gifts compared with what Nordon seems to regard as Doyle's vivid, fictional picture of a Holmes-like Bell showing them off. Nordon goes on:

"Scientific prestige on the one hand and poetic realism on the other made it essential that a model for Sherlock Holmes should be found *a posteriori*, and that that model should be a man of science. We have very little idea what sort of man Joseph Bell really was, for Sherlock Holmes has blurred his outlines. While still a student, and before he had met Bell, the young Conan Doyle had probably begun inventing a rather vague imaginary character; then, when once he had fallen under the spell of his professor's personality, he found it intervening and filling out the details of his fictitious creation."[2]

Professor Nordon could be either right or wrong in what he says in the first sentence of the last quotation. I think, however, that the rest of his speculations, some of which are scarcely complimentary to Doyle, may arise from a lack of full acquaintance with the relevant literature. Let us look, for example, at the suggestion that we are unable to verify the accuracy of Doyle's "Barbados" sketch of Bell because we have so very little independent information about the latter at our disposal.

Twenty years before the publication of *Memories and Adventures*, for example, in an article "The Original of Sherlock Holmes", published in *Colliers* of 9 January, 1904, Harold

[1] Nordon, pp. 213–14. Professor Nordon was awarded the *Prix Guizot* by the Académie Française for the French edition of his book.
[2] Nordon, pp. 214–15.

Emery Jones M.D., a fellow-student of Doyle under Bell, independently recorded demonstrations by Bell identical in style with the Barbados dialogue.[1] John Dickson Carr (whose earlier biography was available to Professor Nordon) has preserved for us two more examples, in the "rich Scots" of Dr. Bell, concerning a left-handed cobbler and a French-polisher.[2] In a further example, the late W. S. Baring-Gould reprinted for our pleasure (also in "rich Scots") the following story of Bell from *The Lancet* of 1 August, 1956, which it is instructive to compare with Doyle's account of the non-commissioned officer from Barbados:

> "A woman with a small child was shown in. Joe Bell said good morning to her and she said good morning in reply.
> 'What sort of a crossing di'ye have fra' Burntisland?'
> 'It was guid.'
> 'And had ye a guid walk up Inverleith Row?'
> 'Yes.'
> 'And what did ye do with th' other wain?'
> 'I left him with my sister in Leith.'
> 'And would ye still be working at the linoleum factory?'
> 'Yes, I am.'
> 'You see, gentlemen, when she said good morning to me I noticed her Fife accent, and, as you know, the nearest town in Fife is Burntisland. You noticed the red clay on the edges of the soles of her shoes, and the only such clay within twenty miles of Edinburgh is in the Botanical Gardens. Inverleigh Row borders the gardens and is her nearest way here from Leith. You observed that the coat she carried over her arm is too big for the child who is with her, and therefore she set out from home with two children. Finally, she has a dermatitis on the fingers of her right hand which is peculiar to the workers in the linoleum factory at Burntisland.' "[3]

[1] These accounts of Bell's identification of three patients respectively as a local fisherman, a cork-cutter or a slater and an alcoholic (as opposed to a sufferer from hip-disease!) are conveniently accessible in Vincent Starrett's *The Private Life of Sherlock Holmes* (London, 1934), pp. 4–6.

[2] Carr, p. 35. Three more independent pen-pictures of Bell's demonstrations of observation and deduction are printed on pp. 35–6 of *Leaves from the Life of a Country Doctor* (*Clement Bryce Gunn, M.D., J.P.*). Edited by Rutherford Crockett, with a Foreword by John Buchan (Edinburgh, 1935). Dr. Gunn was a medical student with Doyle at Edinburgh.

[3] Baring-Gould, *op. cit.*, i, p. 7. One of the best of these stories of Bell is recorded by Mrs. Saxby (*Joseph Bell*, pp. 20–1). Bell observed that a patient "had the whole appearance of a man in one of the Highland regiments". The patient, a shoemaker, retorted that he had never been in the army in his life, a denial which Bell conceded

Professor Nordon's assertion that "we have very little idea what sort of man Joseph Bell really was", also suggests that he is without knowledge of Mrs. J. M. E. Saxby's *Joseph Bell, M.D., F.R.C.S., J.P., D.L. etc. An Appreciation by an Old Friend*, an illustrated biography published in Edinburgh by Oliphant, Anderson and Ferrier in 1913.[1] I am frank to say, too, that in my view Nordon's suggestion that Conan Doyle "while still a student, and before he had met Bell" (and therefore when he was barely seventeen years old) had probably already begun to invent the imaginary character of Sherlock Holmes, has no evidence to support it, and would seem to be demolished by Doyle's own account of the matter, already quoted on page 76.

In June, 1892, Doyle was interviewed at his house in South Norwood by Mr. Harry How, and as a result a long illustrated article "A Day with Dr. Conan Doyle" appeared in *The Strand Magazine* in August of the same year. Doyle was reported as saying:

"[At Edinburgh] I met the man who suggested Sherlock Holmes to me—here is a portrait of him as he was in those days, and he is strong and hearty, and still in Edinburgh . . . His intuitive powers were simply marvellous. Case No. 1 would step up.

'I see', said Mr. Bell, 'you're suffering from drink. You even carry a flask in the inside breast pocket of your coat.' Another case would come forward.

'Cobbler, I see'. Then he would turn to the students, and point out to them that the inside of the knee of the man's trousers was worn. That was where the man had rested the lapstone—a peculiarity only found in cobblers.

All this impressed me very much. He was continually before me— his sharp, piercing grey eyes, eagle nose, and striking features. There he would sit in his chair with fingers together—he was very

"was rather a floorer". When the patient was stripped, however, a small blue "D" branded on his skin was discovered under his left breast. He had been a deserter from the Crimean War, a fact which pride had naturally caused him to wish to conceal.

[1] Jessie Margaret Edmondson Saxby (1842–1914), President of Edinburgh, Orkney and Shetland Literary and Scientific Association, published over thirty volumes of stories, poems and travels. She and her husband, a physician, were lifelong friends of Dr. and Mrs. Bell. Mrs. Saxby's affectionate appreciation of Bell, her last published work, seems to be virtually unknown among writers on Conan Doyle and Sherlock Holmes. In all my years as a book-collector I have only found two copies, one of which I was happy to pass on to my friend the late Lord Donegall.

dextrous with his hands—and just look at the man or woman before him. He was most kind and painstaking with the students—a real good friend—and when I took my degree and went to Africa the remarkable individuality and discriminating tact of my old master made a deep and lasting impression on me, though I had not the faintest idea that it would one day lead me to forsake medicine for writing."

Mr. How went to the trouble of communicating with Dr. Bell, whose letter of 16 June, 1892 in reply was published at the end of "A Day with Dr. Conan Doyle". This letter, which additionally disposes of Professor Nordon's suggestion that we know practically nothing about Dr. Bell's gifts, is of interest and reads in part:

"The recognition [of disease] depends in great measure on the accurate and rapid appreciation of small points in which the diseased differs from the healthy state. In fact the student must be taught to observe. To interest him in this kind of work we teachers find it useful to show the student how much a trained use of observation can discover in ordinary matters such as the previous history, nationality and occupation of a patient. The patient, too, is likely to be impressed by your ability to cure him in the future if he sees that you, at a glance, know much of his past. And the whole trick is much easier than it appears at first.

For instance, physiognomy helps you to nationality, accent to district, and, to an educated ear, almost to county. Nearly every handicraft writes its sign-manual on the hands. The scars of the miner differ from those of the quarryman. The carpenter's callosities are not those of the mason. The shoemaker and the tailor are quite different.

The soldier and the sailor differ in gait—though last month I had to tell a man who said he was a soldier that he had been a sailor in his boyhood. The subject is endless: the tattoo marks on hand and arm will tell their tale as to voyages. The ornaments on the watch chain of the successful settler will tell you where he made his money. A New Zealand squatter will not wear a gold mohur, nor an engineer on an Indian railway a Maori stone. Carry the same idea of using one's senses accurately and constantly, and you will see that many a surgical case will bring his past history, national, social, and medical, into the consulting-room as he walks in."[1]

[1] Mrs. J. M. E. Saxby quoted this letter (with some omissions) on pp. 16–18 of *Joseph Bell*.

In 1893 Ward, Lock & Co. Ltd. re-published *A Study in Scarlet*, presumably because of the renewed demand for the first Sherlock Holmes novel brought about by the publication of the series of short stories in *The Strand Magazine*. As an Introduction to this edition the publishers included (pp. xiii-xx) an essay by Joseph Bell, which had appeared in *The Bookman* earlier in the year, entitled "Mr. Sherlock Holmes".[1] In these pages Bell paid high tribute to his old pupil as "a born story-teller", adding:

> "Dr. Conan Doyle's education as a student of medicine taught him how to observe, and his practice, both as a general practitioner and a specialist, has been a splendid training for a man such as he is, gifted with eyes, memory, and imagination . . . Trained as he has been to notice and appreciate minute detail, Dr. Doyle saw how he could interest his intelligent readers by taking them into his confidence, and showing his mode of working."

Messrs. Ward, Lock & Co., Ltd, in their "Publishers' Note to this Edition" remarked:

> "As it is in *A Study in Scarlet* that Mr. Sherlock Holmes is first introduced to the public, and his methods of work described, it occurred to the publishers of this volume that a paper on "Sherlock Holmes", which Dr. Doyle's old master, Dr. Joseph Bell, the original of Sherlock Holmes, contributed recently to *The Bookman*, would greatly interest readers who did not see it when it appeared in that publication."

Whether Mr. Hesketh Pearson, the author of the controversial *Conan Doyle. His Life and Art*, had seen the whole of the material assembled in the previous pages I do not know. He may have relied in the main on the letter Doyle wrote to him when Pearson warmly reviewed *The Complete Sherlock Holmes Long Stories* in *G.K.'s Weekly* in 1929. Doyle said that in his writings Poe had influenced him and Gaboriau had not, but that more than anyone else Joseph Bell had been responsible for Sherlock Holmes.[2]

Having quoted (I hope fairly) the arguments to the contrary,

---

[1] Professor Nordon refers to this essay as if it had first been published as the Introduction to the "Author's Edition" of the stories in 1903 (Nordon, p. 213, n. 1).

[2] Pearson, p. 186.

I must say now that I agree with Vincent Starrett, one of the earliest and most gifted commentators in this field, who wrote:

"Out of his memories of Joseph Bell, hawk-faced and a trifle eerie for all his sardonic humour, the creator of Sherlock Holmes built the outlines of his great detective. But it was an outline only; it was the special genius of Conan Doyle, himself, that was to enable him to complete the picture. It was from the first, indeed, only the potentialities of *a living Sherlock Holmes latent within his medical creator* [my italics] that made possible the gaunt detective's entrance upon the foggy stage of London's wickedness."[1]

Certainly Joseph Bell himself did not support the all too simple theory that he was the prototype of Sherlock Holmes. In the opening and closing sentences of his published letter of 16 June, 1892, included in the article "A Day with Dr. Conan Doyle", Bell wrote:

"You ask me about the kind of teaching to which Dr. Conan Doyle has so kindly referred, when speaking of his ideal character, "Sherlock Holmes". Dr. Conan Doyle has, by his imaginative genius, made a great deal out of very little, and his warm remembrance of one of his old teachers has coloured the picture . . . Dr. Conan Doyle's generous and intense imagination has on this slender basis made his detective stories a distinctly new departure, but he owes much less than he thinks to yours truly, Joseph Bell."

Bell's private attitude to his identification with Sherlock Holmes, as expressed to his biographer, was one of annoyance. Mrs. Saxby quoted one letter from him in which he wrote:

"Why bother yourself about the cataract of drivel for which Conan Doyle is responsible? I am sure he never imagined that such a heap of rubbish would fall on my devoted head in consequence of his stories."[2]

As a result of this and other comments by Bell Mrs. Saxby was constrained to write:

"When first Conan Doyle's remarkable creation brought its author fame he informed the public that (when a student at Edinburgh) he found the prototype of Sherlock Holmes in his admired professional 'chief', Dr. Joseph Bell. No doubt it is true that the Professor's wonderful gift of quick perception and rapid deductive

---

[1] *The Private Life of Sherlock Holmes*, p. 7.   [2] *Joseph Bell*, p. 14.

reasoning—by which he reached in a flash truths hidden among tangles—gave the clever romancer a suggestion for his great detective's character. But it was only one—and that a subordinate one—of Bell's characteristics which went to the forming of *Sherlock Holmes*.

Rather unfortunately the world was led to understand that the two personalities were identical in every respect, and since Dr. Bell's death in 1911 the Press has unwittingly given more and more weight to the mistaken representation of a good man's personality, and that must be the excuse of one who knew him intimately for now venturing to recall some reminiscences which will show his absolute unlikeness, save in one respect, to Conan Doyle's master-piece."[1]

In this connexion it is perhaps of importance to recall Doyle's original notes on the characteristics of Sherlock Holmes, written early in 1886 when the writing of *A Study in Scarlet* was in active contemplation. It will be remembered that at that time no mention of Dr. Bell was made. "Sherrinford Holmes", as Doyle originally intended to call him, was to be "a sleepy-eyed, reserved young man—collector of rare violins [with a] chemical laboratory", possessed of a private income of four hundred pounds a year, and with "no patience with people who build up fine theories in their own armchairs". It may be thought that this first picture of Holmes (and especially the last phrase) bore no resemblance at all to Joseph Bell. In his notes in 1886 Doyle mentioned, presumably as relevant to what he had in mind, both Gaboriau's Lecoq and Poe's Dupin. Doyle's recollections of Bell were not published until 1892, when the Sherlock Holmes stories had begun to take the world by storm, and their author had already become a literary figure of some importance in consequence. We are entitled to recall in this context Professor Nordon's explanation of the contradictions of 1886 and 1892:

> "Scientific prestige on the one hand and poetic realism on the other made it essential that a model for Sherlock Holmes should be found *a posteriori*, and that that model should be a man of science."[2]

By 1924 Doyle himself was to say that whilst Bell took a keen

---

[1] *Joseph Bell*, pp. 11–12.　　　　　　　　　　[2] Nordon, p. 214.

interest in the Sherlock Holmes stories, the suggestions he made in regard to them were not very practical.[1]

However this may be, there can be no doubt as to Bell's own identification of the real model for Sherlock Holmes. "You are yourself Sherlock Holmes, and well you know it", he wrote to Conan Doyle.[2] In 1924 Doyle himself said:

"I have often been asked whether I had myself the qualities which I depicted, or whether I was merely the Watson that I look. Of course I am well aware that it is one thing to grapple with a practical problem and quite another thing when you are allowed to solve it under your own conditions. I have no delusions about that. At the same time a man cannot spin a character out of his own inner consciousness and make it really life-like unless he has some possibilities of that character within him . . . I find that in real life in order to find [in himself the character of Sherlock Holmes] I have to inhibit all the others and get into a mood when there is no one in the room but he. Then I get results and have several times solved problems by Holmes' methods after the police have been baffled. Yet I must admit that in ordinary life I am by no means observant and that I have to throw myself into an artificial frame of mind before I can weigh evidence and anticipate the sequence of events."[3]

In *The True Conan Doyle* (London, 1945), the late Adrian M. Conan Doyle, who may be presumed to have known his father better than most people, remarked:

"For half a century, a variety of writers and critics have, with insufficient knowledge, confused the public mind by placing all the credit, and not a minor part of that credit, for Sherlock Holmes at the feet of Dr. Joseph Bell, which is analogous to the ridiculous position that could arise if the plaudits due to a brilliant *virtuoso* were reserved only for the teacher who gave him his original music lessons. Conan Doyle was too great in himself to be annoyed by this misconception. Indeed, I know that he derived no small degree of amusement from it . . . Dr. Bell's remarkable characteristics brought to their full growth the deductive propensities latent in Conan Doyle. They did that, and they did no more."[4]

Adrian Conan Doyle added that his father's gifts of deductive observation were unequalled in his son's experience, and probably greater than those of Dr. Bell. However this may be,

[1] *Memories*, p. 26.
[2] Baring-Gould, *op. cit.*, i, p. 8.
[3] *Memories*, pp. 100–1.
[4] *The True Conan Doyle*, pp. 15–16.

one of the most interesting facts recorded in *The True Conan Doyle* (p. 15) is that in 1918 Arthur Conan Doyle told Hayden Coffin, the American journalist, in a private interview, "If anyone is Holmes, then I must confess that it is I".

Professor Nordon devotes nine pages[1] of his biography of Doyle to the proof of "the unmistakable identification between author and hero".[2] He cites the height and physical strength of Doyle and Holmes, their love of boxing and Turkish baths, their chivalry towards women, their enthusiasm for mystification and disguise, their indulgence in untidiness, their horror of destroying documents, their rhythm of work, their attitude to money, their common culture and omnivorous reading (especially Shakespeare, Darwin, Carlyle, Winwood Reade, Meredith, Poe, Goethe, Boileau, La Rochefoucauld, Flaubert and Gaboriau) and their interest in painters of the French school. Nordon points out that both Doyle and Holmes desired the eventual union of the United Kingdom and the United States, that both were offered knighthoods in 1902, that both sprang partly from French descent and partly from lines of country squires, and that both had ancestors who were artists. Both Doyle and Holmes were deeply interested in heredity, in ancient manuscripts and the Cornish language. Nordon reminds us that in *His Last Bow* Holmes chose as a pseudonym "Altamont", the second name of Doyle's father. Nordon concludes the chapter devoted to this theme of positive identification with the following words:

> "In the deepest fibres of his being, his dominant ideas, Holmes is certainly fashioned in Conan Doyle's image. His achievement consists not so much in solving the mystery of appearances as in defending the innocent—we think of the Edalji affair; in righting wrongs—and we think of Slater, the Congo, Divorce reform, Casement; in giving a new value to his creator's ideas of chivalry—and we think of *Sir Nigel* and *The White Company*. In the Adventures, Sherlock Holmes is fighting a spiritual campaign designed to startle consciences and hearts, just as Conan Doyle did in his life. Because he is like Conan Doyle, because he is Conan Doyle, Sherlock Holmes is much more than a portrait: he is one of the last incarnations of chivalry in the literature of the English language."[3]

[1] Nordon, pp. 277–85.   [2] Nordon, p. 285.   [3] Nordon, p. 285.

Michael and Mollie Hardwick, in their little book *The Man who was Sherlock Holmes* (London, 1964), add a few details not mentioned by Nordon. They point out that both Doyle and Holmes liked working in solitude, in old dressing-gowns, and that both indulged in chemical experiments, smoked pipes incessantly and compiled voluminous scrapbooks. They shared the same bankers, and each kept on his desk a magnifying glass and in a drawer, a revolver. Each was a brilliant amateur criminologist, with lessons to teach the official police forces of the world.

Most of these similarities between Doyle and Holmes cited by Nordon and the Hardwicks had already been recorded by John Dickson Carr in *The Life of Sir Arthur Conan Doyle*. In the preparation of this definitive biography Carr had access to a mass of unpublished documents and to the evidence of Doyle's family, circumstances which to the textual critic inevitably make Carr's interpretation of the facts even more convincing than the writings of those who followed in later years and agreed with him. The conclusions he reached cannot therefore be regarded as other than of first importance:

> "Surely it must be obvious that Sherlock Holmes was only himself? The supreme irony was that popular voices who called him by this name—newspapers, hecklers, friends, and countrymen —were perfectly correct. Assuredly he had put enough clues into the stories to show that Holmes was himself. He did not propose to admit the fact publicly; but, sooner or later, he would include a clue so blatantly plain that it could not be missed."[1]

In the last sentence Carr was, of course, referring to *His Last Bow*, first published in *The Strand Magazine* of September, 1917. Whilst, as he remarked, Doyle had slipped many "deliberate identifications of Holmes" with himself into the earlier stories, it was in the unusually emotional *His Last Bow* that the final revelation was contained:

> "Even without our private knowledge of the author's state of mind, we can feel in the texture of *His Last Bow* that it is more than another adventure of Sherlock Holmes. It was, as the author sub-titled it, an 'epilogue'. It was to be, really and finally, *His Last Bow*.

[1] Carr, p. 200.

There is foreboding in it; and true emotion, and towards Holmes, a strong touch of affection. In it Conan Doyle at last identified Holmes with himself . . . It is the last thrill, the final drum-beat, the apotheosis of Sherlock Holmes. The whole series should have ended with *His Last Bow*, as the author formally and finally intended it to end. It was identification too. To Sherlock Holmes in disguise he gave the name of 'Altamont'; and the full name of his father, we remember, was Charles Altamont Doyle."[1]

For me at least, the matter is settled by the fact that John Dickson Carr wrote of the identification with the advantage of original sources[2] at his disposal:

" 'Why don't you tell them?' Jean [Lady Conan Doyle] would urge him, over and over. She, to whom he had confided the truth so many years ago, never ceased urging it.[3] And yet, though he so strongly hinted at it in his autobiography, Holmes's identity remained his secret joke."[4]

It will be seen from the foregoing pages that there is at least one student of the literature of Baker Street who is at amiable variance with Michael Harrison in his positive identification of Sherlock Holmes as Wendel Scherer, despite the attractive originality of the idea. I am also of the opinion that the unqualified acceptance of Dr. Joseph Bell as the prototype of Holmes is an over-simplification of the problem, despite its support by writers like John Lamond, Howard Haycraft and Hesketh Pearson. I find myself in agreement with John Dickson Carr, Vincent Starrett and Adrian Conan Doyle in the convinced belief that the true Sherlock Holmes was almost wholly a reflection of the genius of his creator, but with the hawk-like face of Dr. Joseph Bell glancing round the rim of the mirror. I hope that I have assembled the evidence fairly, and have possibly added here and there to its documentation.

[1] Carr, pp. 315–17.
[2] "Correspondence is the only true breath of life. Memories blur. Even a man's autobiography hesitates as it gropes back. But *there*, shut up in old papers, is the living emotion; *that* was what he felt at the time, when the blood ran fast, that is the truth." (Carr, p. 9).
[3] Lady Conan Doyle's knowledge of the matter was confirmed four years after her husband's death in her article "Conan Doyle was Sherlock Holmes" in *Pearson's Magazine*, December, 1934.
[4] Carr, p. 330.

VIII

CONAN DOYLE AND SPIRITUALISM

STANDARD biographical dictionaries and works of literary reference seem to touch with purposeful lightness upon the subject matter of this essay. Thus, in Doyle's seventeen-line entry in the second volume (1901–1950) of *The Concise Dictionary of National Biography* (London, 1961) his deep interest in spiritualism in his later years is dealt with in a single phrase. Although Doyle's published psychic books numbered more than a dozen, only his *The History of Spiritualism* (London, 1926) is mentioned in the twenty-six lines devoted to his literary work in Sir Paul Harvey's *The Oxford Companion to English Literature* (Third Edition, London, 1946). This reluctance by some to acknowledge the fact that the last fourteen years of Doyle's life[1] were dominated by his devotion to spiritualism would seem to echo the view of Doyle's first biographer, the Rev. John Lamond, in regard to Doyle's contemporaries:

> "They appreciated and loved Arthur Conan Doyle, the author of *Sherlock Holmes* and *The White Company*. They deprecated the fact that he ever espoused the cause of Spiritualism. The writings of the last twelve years of his life[2] they would willingly ignore."[3]

Some other writers have not displayed a similar reticence. In the *New York Times* of 2 September, 1923, a formidable attack on Sir Arthur Conan Doyle was published over the signature of Professor Joseph Jastrow, Professor of Psychology

[1] Doyle announced his conversion to spiritualism in 1916. He died in 1930.
[2] Doyle's first psychic book, *The New Revelation*, was published in London in 1918.
[3] Lamond, p. 249.

in the University of Wisconsin, of which the following is a part:

"It is very easy to show that Sir Arthur has been repeatedly and grossly deceived by the most vulgar kind of spirit-séance that is designed to prey upon the emotions of the gullible. He has subscribed to the genuineness of frauds that have been repeatedly exposed to the last detail of ingenious or clumsy deception . . . In brief, if there is any one member of the very small modern group of distinguished men who for one reason or another have gone over to the delusion of the supernormal, who is thoroughly discredited by his versatile and eager credulity and his readiness to ignore all the exposure of fraud that has been accumulated, it is Sir Arthur Conan Doyle."

It is proper to recall in this context that for many years Professor Jastrow had been a determined and extreme opponent of spiritualism and so-called psychical research. At the turn of the century he had written:

"The phenomena now associated with modern Spiritualism, with their characteristic *milieu,* breed the typical atmosphere of the séance chamber which resists precise analysis, but which in its extreme form involves morbid credulity, blind prepossession, and emotional contagion; while the dependence of the phenomena on the character of the medium offers strong temptation alike to shrewdness, eccentricity, and dishonesty . . . Just so long as a portion of mankind will accept material evidence of such a belief, and will even countenance the irreverence, the triviality, and the vulgarity surrounding the manifestations; just so long as those persons will misjudge their own powers of detecting how the alleged supernatural appearances are really produced, and remain unimpressed by the principles upon which alone a consistent explanation is possible, just so long will Spiritualism and kindred delusions flourish . . . If one may judge by the tone and contents of current spiritualistic literature, the rank and file to which Spiritualism appeals present an unintellectual occult company, credulously accepting what they wish to believe, utterly regardless of the intrinsic significance of evidence or hypothesis, vibrating from one extreme or absurdity to another, and blindly following a blinder or more fanatic leader or a self-interested charlatan."[1]

Of psychical research Professor Jastrow wrote in the same place:

---

[1] Joseph Jastrow, *Fact and Fable in Psychology* (London, 1901), pp. 15–16.

"The influence which Psychical Research has cast in favour of the occult, the enrolment under a common protective authority of the credulous and the superstitious, and the believers in mystery and in the personal significance of things, is but one of the evils that must be laid at its door. Equally pernicious is the distorted conception, which the prominence of Psychical Research has scattered broadcast, of the purposes and methods of Psychology. The status of that science has suffered, its representatives have been misunderstood, its advancement has been hampered, its appreciation by the public at large has been weakened and wrongly estimated, by reason of the popularity of the unfortunate aspects of Psychical Research, and of its confusion with them. Whatever in the publications of Psychical Research seems to favour mystery and to substantiate supernormal powers is readily absorbed, and its bearings fancifully interpreted and exaggerated; the more critical and successfully explanatory papers meet with a less extended and less sensational reception."[1]

The same charge of foolish gullibility was brought against the creator of Sherlock Holmes by Dr. George Lawton, despite the more temperate phrasing and the emphasis upon Doyle's fine character:

"An excellent example of the layman researcher was Sir A. C. Doyle. Setting aside for the moment his extraordinary and most lovable personal qualities, his literary genius, the chief qualification that he possessed for the rôle of investigator was his crusading zeal. Among all the notable persons attracted to Spiritualism he was perhaps the most uncritical."[2]

A criticism published ten years ago, by the late Simeon Edmunds, did not differ in content from those already quoted, thus spanning a period of more than forty years:

"His extreme credulity, indeed, was the despair of his colleagues, all of whom, however, held him in the highest respect for his complete honesty. From the end of the First World War until his death, Doyle devoted the great part of his time and energy to the cause of spiritualism."[3]

[1] *Op. cit.*, pp. 75–6.
[2] *The Drama of Life after Death. A Study of the Spiritualist Religion* (London, 1933), p. 534.
[3] *Spiritualism. A Critical Survey* (London, 1966), pp. 15–16.

Although Edmunds emphasised the respect in which Doyle was universally held by commentators on spiritualism and psychical research, the late Dr. W. F. Prince went near to accusing the creator of Sherlock Holmes of lack of honesty in his presentation of the evidence for the reality of occult phenomena. Prince was discussing the collision between the book, *A Magician Among the Spirits* (New York and London, 1924) by the illusionist Harry Houdini, one of the foremost and most violent of critics of spiritualism, and Doyle's own *The History of Spiritualism* (London, 1926). In the year of Doyle's death, Prince wrote:

"Doyle correctly says that Houdini 'stuffed so many errors into his book' and 'has shown extraordinary bias on the whole question'. But the errors which stare you in the face [in *A Magician Among the Spirits*] were not wilful ones, since few of them were of any advantage to the argument. And bias is less reprehensible in a book which professes from the beginning to the end to be an assault, than it would be in what professes to be a history . . . It would have been strange if the university man and trained physician [Doyle] had committed so many perfectly obvious blunders of fact and citation, as we have noted in the book written by the man [Houdini] who had to launch out and earn his own living when he was a mere boy. But Sir Arthur was not by any means so immune from palpable misstatements as he on several occasions intimated to the public was the case. Yet on careful comparison, one is impressed by one peculiar difference—the mistakes of Houdini very frequently do not help his argument—that is, if he had got the facts straight they would have served his type of propaganda just as much, while Sir Arthur's blunders nearly always work to the favor of his argument. It is not to be understood that the latter deliberately misrepresented the facts, but that his intense zeal in behalf of a cause, his burning wish that the 'phenomena' should be vindicated, colored his mental vision and disturbed his judgment to the point that he did not always mentally grasp sentences actually before him in print, or appreciate the overwhelming preponderance of evidence."[1]

At this point it may be helpful to recall Doyle's case on behalf of spiritualism. Three years before his death, in a symposium of views for and against psychical belief, Doyle stated his own

---

[1] Walter Franklin Prince, *The Enchanted Boundary, being a Survey of Negative Reactions to Claims of Psychic Phenomena, 1820–1930* (Boston, 1930), pp. 150–3.

position under a chapter heading, "THE PSYCHIC QUESTION AS I SEE IT":

"I consider [spiritualism] to be infinitely the most important thing in the world, and the particular thing which the human race in its present state of development needs more than anything else. Nothing is secure until the religious basis is secure, and that spiritualistic movement with which I am proud to be associated is the first attempt ever made in modern times to support faith by actual provable fact.

I would first state my credentials, since my opinion is only of value in so far as these are valid. In 1886, being at that time a materialist, I was induced to examine psychic phenomena. In 1887 I wrote a signed article in *Light* upon the question. From that time I have never ceased to keep in touch with the matter by reading and occasional experiment. My conversion to the full meaning of spiritualism was a very gradual one, but by the war time it was complete. In 1916 I gave a lecture upon the subject, and found that it gave strength and comfort to others. I therefore determined to devote all my time to it, and so in the last ten years I have concentrated on it, testing very many mediums, good and bad, studying the extensive literature, keeping in close touch with current psychic research, and incidentally writing seven books on the subject. It is not possible that any living man can have had a much larger experience. When I add that I am a Doctor of medicine, specially trained in observation, and that as a public man of affairs I have never shown myself to be wild or unreasonable, I hope I have persuaded you that my opinion should have some weight as compared with those opponents whose contempt for the subject has been so great that it has prevented them from giving calm consideration to the facts."[1]

It is valuable to have available to us Doyle's own assessment of the reasons for his devotion to spiritualism, and I shall discuss later in this essay the significance of his own statement that prior to 1916 his experience seems to have been limited to "reading and occasional experiment". In two of his books, the late Harry Price described Doyle's involvement with spiritualism not unsympathetically, from the former's position as an observer and an acquaintance of many years. It can scarcely be denied,

[1] Carl Murchison (Ed.) *The Case for and Against Psychical Belief* (Worcester, Massachusetts, 1927), p. 15.

however, that the overall impression created by both Price's views and most of the earlier comments I have quoted is that in regard to spiritualism, the creator of Sherlock Holmes was sincere but exceedingly simple and credulous. Price wrote in 1939:

> "Conan Doyle, sincere, lovable, credulous, was a propagandist of a different type. He made no pretence to studying phenomena from the scientific angle . . . Immediately after the war he became an active propagandist and during the ten years from 1920 until his death, he lectured [on spiritualism] in Australasia, the United States, South Africa and Northern Europe. His tours brought him money, but it is probable that, owing to his activities in the cause of spiritualism, he was thousands of pounds out of pocket. He sat with many mediums, some of whom deceived him. Thoroughly honest himself, he could not imagine his too sympathetic credulity being imposed upon."[1]

In his later autobiography, writing of the "Exhibition of Objects of Psychic Interest" at the National Laboratory of Psychical Research in 1925, Price said:

> "The Exhibition was particularly rich in 'spirit' photographs, and Sir A. Conan Doyle sent a large collection, every one of which was, apparently, a fake! Poor, dear, lovable, credulous Doyle!"[2]

Later in the same book Price wrote:

> "Doyle died on July 7, 1930, in his seventy-second year, and the spiritualists lost the greatest personality the movement ever possessed, or is likely to possess. By sheer personal domination he raised the subject of psychic phenomena into the arena of acute controversy—and kept it there. A born fighter, sometimes intolerant, and often open to criticism (as when he championed those ridiculous Cottingley fairies[3]), there was hardly a journal in the country to which he did not contribute some of his stunning arguments for the reality of a spiritual world. Lovable and large-hearted to a degree, this very quality was often taken advantage of by the unscrupulous rogues who abused his ever-ready friendship. Too honest himself, he could not imagine his sympathetic credulity being imposed upon. He was a giant in stature with the heart of a

[1] *Fifty Years of Psychical Research* (London, 1939), p. 309.
[2] *Search for Truth. My Life for Psychical Research* (London, 1942), p. 90.
[3] Sir Arthur Conan Doyle, *The Coming of the Fairies* (London, 1922).

child. It is doubtful if anyone will ever take Doyle's place. I do not know of another spiritualist living with the same dynamic personality, driving-force, dogged grit, tenacity of purpose, fighting qualities and world-wide prestige that this great High Priest of Spiritualism possessed. Often he has told me that it was his ambition that he should go down to posterity as the exponent of a great religion, rather than as the creator of 'Sherlock Holmes', and the other characters that his vivid imagination and facile pen have immortalised for us. But posterity will disappoint him, I am afraid. The spiritualists themselves have almost forgotten him, and have not even troubled to establish a memorial to his memory. And no good biography of this great man has yet appeared.[1] No, Doyle will be remembered as a writer of fiction, not as a spiritualist."[2]

* * *

John Carter once wrote that a critic has a duty to define his terms of reference and to present his credentials before presuming upon his readers' attention.[3] In this essay I am offering my personal views upon the startling fact (to many) that during the last fourteen years of his life Conan Doyle, the creator of Sherlock Holmes, became the most famous convert to spiritualism in the history of that movement, and its most vigorous propagandist. It is, I think, unfortunate that earlier writers, possibly better qualified than I am to comment upon this puzzle, have tended to avoid doing so or have sharply disagreed with each other. Thus, the late Adrian Conan Doyle was frank to say that he did not intend to discuss his father's championship of spiritualism, other than to observe that Doyle studied the subject for thirty-three years before devoting the remainder of his life to it.[4]

Doyle's first biographer, John Lamond, did not consider that he was confronted by any problem in this connexion. To Lamond, a convinced and active believer, it evidently seemed entirely

---

[1] When this was written, only John Lamond's *Arthur Conan Doyle. A Memoir* had appeared. Six later biographies of Doyle were to be published.

[2] *Search for Truth*, pp. 262–3.

[3] *Taste & Technique in Book-Collecting* (Cambridge, 1948), p. ix.

[4] *The True Conan Doyle* (London, 1945), p. 18. Adrian Conan Doyle did not become a spiritualist, despite his mother's forecast during an interview with Lady Doyle reported in the *Sheffield Daily Telegraph* of 22 July, 1930. "My sons, Adrian and Dennis, have finished their University careers, and are going to follow in their father's footsteps and devote their lives to the spread of psychic knowledge."

natural that a man of Doyle's character, intelligence and training, should enthusiastically embrace spiritualism as a religion. To John Dickson Carr, however, generally regarded as Doyle's definitive biographer, the puzzle presented by Doyle as a spiritualist was an obvious one:

"For a quarter of a century he had loomed thick-shouldered as the sturdy Briton, with no damned nonsense about him. What was wrong? What ailed the man?"[1]

Hesketh Pearson, on the other hand, offered an explanation which to some may seem sufficient, and to others too simple to be the whole answer:

"Doyle's nature demanded a religion. The Jesuits had disgusted him with their hell-fire nonsense,[2] and he was too rational to accept any of the ready-made creeds. He therefore began in his Southsea days to look about for something that would harmonise with his temperament and appeal to his reason."[3]

It is fair to point out that Pearson's account of Doyle was not accepted by at least two later writers. The late Adrian Conan Doyle, for example, said of Conan Doyle. His Life and Art:

"In its portrayal of my father and his opinions, the book is a travesty and the personal values therein ascribed to him are, in effect, the very antithesis of everything that he represented, believed in and held dear."[4]

Pearson's biography was severely criticised, too, by Pierre Nordon, who in Conan Doyle asserted that Pearson was guilty of "ridiculous inferences", and of reducing literary criticism to "a puerile caricature".[5] These strictures were extended by Nordon to include both Dr. John Lamond and John Dickson

[1] Carr, p. 323.
[2] There is support for this assertion from Doyle himself, who wrote in his autobiography, "I heard Father Murphy, a great fierce Irish priest, declare that there was sure damnation for everyone outside the Church. I looked upon him with horror, and to that moment I trace the first rift which has grown into such a chasm between me and those who were my guides" (Memories, pp. 20–1). The coolness was mutual. When Doyle died it was stated frigidly in the Catholic Times of July, 1930, "It is reported to us that the late Sir Arthur, while at Stonyhurst was a Catholic, though he did not exhibit much faith and did not frequent the Sacraments. It is believed that he subsequently went to another Catholic college before becoming a stranger to Catholicism. Of the circumstances of his early life we have no knowledge, and we regret the necessity to comment on the subject."
[3] Pearson, p. 172.   [4] The True Conan Doyle, p. 5.   [5] Nordon, p. 274.

Carr in regard to their treatment of the delicate matter of Doyle's conversion to spiritualism. Nordon wrote of Lamond's *Arthur Conan Doyle. A Memoir* that "it suggests in an extremely inexplicit manner that he had experienced some form of revelation, without going into the psychological factors which prepared the way for it".[1] Of Carr's *The Life of Sir Arthur Conan Doyle* he remarked:

> "On the other hand Conan Doyle's second biographer, Mr. John Dickson Carr, was much too reticent about the spiritualistic phase, which is all the more to be regretted because he was a great deal better informed than his predecessor as to the reasons for Sir Arthur Conan Doyle's adherence to spiritualism. While Lamond devotes two thirds of his book to the question, Mr. Dickson Carr uses his own incredulous attitude to spiritualism as a pretext for declining to give an opinion and gives barely a twentieth of his book to it."[2]

The question as to whether these particular criticisms are well-founded need not detain us. It is, I think, sufficient for my purpose to have documented the fact that differences of opinion do exist between some of Doyle's biographers on the question before us, and that an examination of the evidence is justified.

As to my credentials, I made it clear in the Preface of my first book on Sherlock Holmes that I was a devotee of Conan Doyle, and that I was permanently indebted to the "indestructible genius of that great Englishman". I added:

> "As a boy and already a Holmes enthusiast, I had the good fortune to be introduced to Sir Arthur by my late father, and even after the passage of over forty years some of the pleasure and excitement of that conversation has remained with me to heighten almost a lifetime's enjoyment of the narratives themselves."[3]

I have assembled with affection a sizeable Doyle collection, including every biography and as much of the related material as I have been able to find. My Holmes first editions are among the most treasured items in my entire library, which embraces more than one subject. It will be understood, therefore, that as an admirer of Conan Doyle as a man and a writer, the criticisms

---

[1] Nordon, p. 139.
[2] Nordon, p. 139. Carr was Doyle's fourth biiographer.
[3] Hall (1), p. v.

of him that I have quoted earlier in this essay are not pleasing. I hope to show that they may be answered.

On the other hand, as Dr. E. J. Dingwall wrote some years ago, I precipitated upon myself a "torrent of criticism and abuse" from believers in spiritualism,[1] because I published a book[2] and a supplement to it[3] casting grave doubts upon the genuineness of the notorious Victorian materialising medium Florence Cook, and the good faith of her sponsor, the scientist William Crookes. I was one of the three unpopular exposers of the mass of credulity, muddled thinking and plain fraud of which the story of Borley Rectory, "the most haunted house in England", mainly consisted.[4] I have written four other books, one also jointly with Dr. Dingwall and one in collaboration with Dr. John Lorne Campbell of Canna, all of which have been critical of the claims of the spiritualists and their fellow-travellers, who include a high percentage of psychical researchers.[5] I am, to put the matter mildly, not a believer in occultism. It has in consequence been urged upon me that out of the presumed conflict of my devotion to Doyle as a writer and a man on the one hand, and my critical view of spiritualism on the other, some kind of balanced opinion might conceivably emerge. Such an investigation has the special attraction that Sherlock Holmes inevitably has a part to play.

*　　*　　*

Both Carr[6] and Nordon[7] said that the date of Doyle's conversion to spiritualism as a religion occurred between September, 1915, and January, 1916. Doyle himself said that he began his campaign "in 1916".[8] For what it is worth, my opinion is that there is something to be said for a date of October, 1916, when Doyle announced his belief in communication with the dead in the spiritualist magazine *Light*. However this may be, 1916

---

[1] *The Critics' Dilemma* (Crowhurst, 1966), p. 73.

[2] *The Spiritualists. The Story of Florence Cook and William Crookes* (London, 1962).

[3] *Florence Cook and William Crookes. A Footnote to an Enquiry* (London, 1963).

[4] E. J. Dingwall, K. M. Goldney and T. H. Hall, *The Haunting of Borley Rectory. A Critical Survey of the Evidence* (London, 1956).

[5] *Four Modern Ghosts* (London, 1958) with Dr. E. J. Dingwall, *The Strange Case of Edmund Gurney* (London, 1964), *New Light on Old Ghosts* (London, 1965) and *Strange Things* (London, 1968) with Dr. J. L. Campbell.

[6] Carr, p. 305.　　　　　　[7] Nordon, p. 156.　　　　　　[8] *Memories*, p. 396.

was the beginning of the last phase of Doyle's life, ending with his death in 1930. He said of this period that spiritualism had now become to him the most important subject in the world, and that he was determined to devote to its propagation, either by pen or voice, the whole of his talents and remaining energy.[1] Of the implications of this milestone in Doyle's life Carr wrote:

"He would be the most famous convert to Spiritualism, the target for everybody, because he was the most incredible convert. Then, of course, there was the question of money . . . He must write little except psychic books, psychic articles, psychic arguments. If he lectured, he could accept only his expenses in payment."[2]

During this last phase of his life from 1916 to 1930 Doyle accomplished the enormous task of publishing thirteen books on spiritualism,[3] concurrently with the writing of his auto-biography, in addition to an outpouring from his pen of in-numerable articles on psychic matters and the heavy labour of his extensive lecture tours. In the same period, however (the arithmetical coincidence is curious) no less than thirteen new Sherlock Holmes stories were published, nearly a quarter of the total series of fifty-six shorter pieces which had commenced with *A Scandal in Bohemia* in 1891.[4] This contradictory circumstance of Doyle's apparent continuing devotion to Holmes throughout the years of his life dedicated to spiritualism did not pass unnoticed by Carr:

"Was there a meeting to be attended? A medium to be investi-gated? A speech to be made? A controversy to be fought, privately or in the press? There he walked, with his umbrella and his towering presence; and with him, at a few odd times in the 'Strand', walked Sherlock Holmes. From *The Adventure of the Mazarin Stone* in

[1] *Memories*, pp. 395 and 408.   [2] Carr, p. 323.
[3] *The New Revelation*, 1918; *The Vital Message*, 1919; *The Wanderings of a Spiritualist*, 1921; *The Case for Spirit Photography*, 1922; *The Coming of the Fairies*, 1922; *Our American Adventure*, 1923; *Our Second American Adventure*, 1924; *The Spiritualist's Reader*, 1924; *The Land of Mist*, 1926; *The History of Spiritualism*, 1926; *Pheneas Speaks*, 1927; *Our African Winter*, 1929, and *The Edge of the Unknown*, 1930.
[4] It follows that the comment by Sherman Yellen, "The Great War, nevertheless must list one casualty who was inextricably connected with Conan Doyle's life; it claimed Sherlock Holmes as its victim. After Verdun, there could be no easy return to Baker Street" (*International Journal of Parapsychology*, New York, Winter, 1965, vii, No. 1, p. 42), has no foundation in fact.

1921 to *The Adventure of Shoscombe Old Place* in 1927, he did not abandon his old companion.''[1]

Just as Carr recognised that there was an apparent contradiction in Doyle continuing to publish Sherlock Holmes stories during this last part of his life, which he said was to be entirely devoted to spiritualism, Carr saw, too, the complementary puzzle that Doyle "even went out of his way to make Holmes deny all belief in the supernatural".[2] Carr's suggested explanation is, however, too simple in my opinion. It was that "Holmes —whom he had set up as a calculating-machine—must click with absolute consistency, like a machine, from beginning to end".[3] This is not entirely convincing, for Holmes was very far from being just a calculating machine, and was by no means always consistent.

Michael and Mollie Hardwick, more or less on the same point, offered a theory of their own. They said that if Doyle had made Holmes his personal mouthpiece for spiritualism, "about which he cared so passionately . . . there would certainly have followed a wave of interest and support. Conan Doyle's artistic integrity forbade him."[4] The assumption contained in the last sentence is, I fear, demolished by a simple factual comparison. When Doyle published *The Land of Mist* in 1926, his "artistic integrity" did not prevent him making the whole theme of the book the complete conversion of Professor Challenger of *The Lost World* (second only to Holmes and perhaps Brigadier Gerard in popularity) from previous scientific scepticism to absolute belief in communication with the dead. Carr wrote of it:

"Many people did not like the book because they did not like its theme. Challenger was fallen from his glory of warring monsters, when only so recently as '23 he had romped through one of the best of all motion pictures in the film-version of *The Lost World*. 'Conan Doyle is preaching!' exclaimed so many; and of course he was.''[5]

[1] Carr, pp. 329–30. This was not quite right. *The Mazarin Stone*, first published in *The Strand Magazine* in October, 1921, was one of the twelve stories later published in book form in 1927 as *The Case-Book of Sherlock Holmes*. *His Last Bow*, however, first published in September, 1917, comes into the period and precedes *The Mazarin Stone*, thus making up the baker's dozen.
[2] Carr, p. 330.   [3] Carr, p. 330.
[4] *The Man who was Sherlock Holmes* (London, 1964), pp. 89–90.
[5] Carr, p. 331.

This criticism, if it was intended as a criticism, must be regarded as well-founded. Poor Challenger, mourning the loss of his wife, is pictured throughout *The Land of Mist*, with the exception of the last two chapters, as a violent but ignorant opponent of spiritualism. He is furious when his daughter Enid and his old companion Edward Malone, who have fallen in love, embrace the spiritualist faith. He opposes their marriage. In the penultimate chapter of the book Enid, who has developed mediumistic powers, delivers two messages to Challenger while in a trance which convince him of the reality of communication with the dead. He becomes an ardent spiritualist and all ends happily.

Doyle's narrative power enlivens *The Land of Mist* here and there by accounts of a dangerously haunted house (which is exorcised by a courageous clergyman who is also a spiritualist), the materialisation of a Pithecanthropus, and a public debate on spiritualism in which Challenger (through lack of knowledge of the subject) suffers a humiliating defeat at the hands of a Mr. Smith.[1] These diversions apart, it seems impossible to contradict Professor Nordon's critical assessment of *The Land of Mist* as simply "an apologia for spiritualism in novel form".[2] The fact that only one edition after the first was published shows that even the devotees of the most popular short-story writer in the world were not attracted by the chapters of *The Land of Mist* describing séances and spiritualist meetings, and the supposed persecution of mediums by unscrupulous police and biased and ignorant magistrates. At the end of the book the once heroic and eccentric Challenger, now converted, is described as "a gentler, humbler and more spiritual man . . . his great brain growing even stronger and more virile as it faces such problems as the future had in store—a future which had ceased to be bounded by the narrow horizon of death, and which now stretched away into the infinite possibilities and developments of continual survival of personality, character and work".[3]

If, by contrast, one glances almost anywhere among the

---

[1] Doubtless inspired by *A Public Debate on "The Truth of Spiritualism"* between *Sir Arthur Conan Doyle, M.D., LL.D. (representing Spiritualism) and Joseph McCabe (representing the Rationalist Press Association)* (London, 1920). This pamphlet was a printed report of a contest that was, in fact, indecisive.

[2] Nordon, p. 333.   [3] *The Land of Mist*, pp. 281–2.

crackling prose of the eternally popular *The Lost World* or *The Hound of the Baskervilles* it is not difficult to understand why there were no comparable streams of later editions and issues of *The Land of Mist*. Sherman Yellen wrote of it with (in my opinion) unnecessary severity, but not without some foundation in fact:

> "*The Land of Mist* demonstrates that Conan Doyle had made his greatest sacrifice to his Spiritualist beliefs; he had relinquished his literary power to it. Indeed, the book is dreadful as literature, and even weaker as Spiritualist propaganda. Whereas the most weakly argued of his non-fiction Spiritualist publications reveals a mastery of style and firm narrative power, now Conan Doyle's prose falters; the dialogue is ludicrous, the characterisations are non-existent."[1]

The publication of Doyle's writings about Sherlock Holmes was spread over precisely forty years, more than half his life, and it is a curious coincidence that 1887, the year of Sherlock Holmes's debut in *A Study in Scarlet*, was also the year when Doyle's interest in spiritualism was first awakened, a date he himself indicated in 1918 in his first psychic book.[2] Those were the days when he was practising medicine in Southsea, and one of his most impressive patients, General Drayson, a firm believer in spirit return and communication, had introduced the young doctor to the subject. Doyle described Drayson as "a very distinguished thinker and pioneer of psychic knowledge, who lived at that time in Southsea".[3]

Major-General Alfred Wilkes Drayson, R.A.,[4] who had retired from the army in 1883 with the rank of colonel, was born in 1827 and was therefore thirty-two years older than Doyle, who was in his late twenties at this period. It seems

---

[1] *International Journal of Parapsychology*, New York, Winter, 1965, vii, No. 1, p. 53.

[2] *The New Revelation* (London, 1918), pp. 16–27.

[3] *Pearson's Magazine*, March, 1924, p. 204. Doyle contributed two long illustrated articles on his experiences in spiritualism to this periodical in March and April, 1924, respectively entitled "Early Psychic Experiences" and "What Comes After Death", totalling 18 pages in all. It is odd that neither of his bibliographers, Harold Locke and Pierre Nordon (who remarked critically that Locke's work contained "a certain number of gaps"), mention these two quite important essays.

[4] It is odd that Lamond, two-thirds of whose biography of Doyle was devoted to his career as a spiritualist, should be incapable of reproducing correctly the name of the man who first introduced Doyle to the subject. In both his text and index Lamond without exception refers to "General Grayson" (Lamond, pp. 34, 35, 36 and 307).

entirely possible that Drayson's seniority in age was an ingredient in the favourable impression he made on the young physician. Drayson had published a curious book purporting to prove that the earth was constantly growing larger,[1] which had attracted some critical attention but to which Doyle attached importance. It is, however, noteworthy that although Drayson first aroused Doyle's interest in spiritualism, he was not successful in converting him to belief in it. Doyle wrote in 1924:

"His opinion, therefore, was not negligible on any subject, and when he told me his views and experiences on Spiritualism I could not fail to be impressed, though my own philosophy was far too solid to be easily destroyed."[2]

Whatever experiences in spiritualism General Drayson may have recounted to Doyle during the latter's Southsea days (Doyle moved to 12 Tennison Road, South Norwood at the end of 1890) there can be no doubt that some of Drayson's later psychic claims under the pseudonym of "General Lorrison"[3] were remarkable, to say the least of it:

"In *Light* for 1895 (pp. 283, 295, 355), there is an account of some extraordinary apport[3] phenomena which occurred during a considerable period in the private circle of General 'Lorrison' of Portsmouth.[5] The General stated that he had thousands of apports of all kinds including eggs, fruit, and vegetables. The eggs came in abundance, from one to two dozen every week, so that none had to be bought for the household. The controls brought them, they said, from Brooklyn, New York, as a gift from a spirit circle to which General 'Lorrison' sent return gifts in a similar way."[6]

Of this story of Drayson's in the years subsequent to his

---

[1] *The Earth We Inhabit, its past, present, and probable future* (London, 1859). In a warm review of the book in *The British Spiritual Telegraph* of 1 April, 1859, it was said, "We believe that the first suggestion of this problem was a spiritual communication". In the same year General Drayson published another book, *Great Britain has been and will be again within the Tropics*.

[2] *Pearson's Magazine*, March, 1924, p. 205.

[3] " 'Lorrison' was the *nom-de-plume* of Major-General A. W. Drayson, a distinguished writer on various scientific subjects and an experienced psychic researcher." (*Light*, 1901, p. 475).

[4] An "apport" (in occult nomenclature) is an object which is alleged to materialize during a spiritualist séance.

[5] Portsmouth and Southsea are contiguous.

[6] A. Campbell Holms, *The Facts of Psychic Science and Philosophy* (London, 1925), p. 356.

acquaintance with Doyle, the late Sir Oliver Lodge, who was not generally critical of the claims of spiritualism, under the heading "General Lorrison's Eggs from New York" wrote in 1897:

> "The next upshot would appear to be that the General acquired by spiritual parcel post some American eggs which his own hens might just as well have laid, and some New England fruit which might equally well have been bought in the market at home. I venture to think either that the event did not happen, or that if it did happen it was wasted for humanity."[1]

Since this incident was first reported in the spiritualist press in 1895, it is clear that Doyle was not regaled with it during his Southsea acquaintance with Drayson. I have assembled the facts, with emphasis on the dates, because Drayson's name in psychic literature is generally associated (a) with his arousing of Doyle's interest in spiritualism and (b) the ridiculous story of the eggs.[2] The two incidents were separated in time by at least five years. In view of the many published assertions that Doyle was exceedingly credulous in psychic matters, it would seem to be important to show that there is no evidence to suggest that Drayson's "spiritual parcel post" of eggs and vegetables played any part in causing Doyle first to become interested in spiritualism.

Returning to Southsea and 1887, there was a good reason why Doyle's state of mind at this period would be exceedingly receptive to the attractions of spiritualism. Strictly educated at Hodder, Stonyhurst and Feldkirch in the Roman Catholic faith of his family, Doyle had finally rejected it, as we have seen. He said himself that like many young medical men, he now found himself amidst the conflict of being a convinced materialist as regards belief in any personal destiny on the one hand, whilst remaining an earnest theist on the other. "This was my frame of mind when Spiritual phenomena first came before my notice", he confessed.[3]

---

[1] *Borderland*, April, 1897, iv, No. 2, p. 165.

[2] It is unfortunate that Doyle's first biographer wrote that during the period of the séances with "General Grayson and his family" Doyle's interest was most aroused by the apports of eggs. "It was these *apports* that puzzled the young doctor" (Lamont, pp. 35–6).

[3] *The New Revelation*, pp. 17–19.

Doyle began to read books like William Crookes's *Researches in the Phenomena of Spiritualism* (London, 1874) and Alfred Russel Wallace's *On Miracles and Modern Spiritualism* (London, 1875), and with the encouragement of General Drayson, to attend séances with a local medium named Horstead. It is perhaps typical of Doyle as an author that he kept records of these sittings and some experiments in telepathy, and even contributed an account of some of his earliest experiences in a letter published in the spiritualist paper *Light* on 2 July, 1887. One result of this was that he was approached by the poet F. W. H. Myers,[1] who with W. F. Barrett, Henry Sidgwick and Edmund Gurney had founded the Society for Psychical Research in 1882, and the two men began to correspond. Myers urged Doyle to help the S.P.R. in its researches, but it was not until 1893, after Doyle had moved from No. 1, Bush Villas, Southsea to No. 12 Tennison Road, South Norwood and had forsaken medicine to live entirely by his writings, that he actually became a member of the Society.[2] Doyle's recollection that he joined the S.P.R. "about 1891" was two years too early.[3]

To most earlier writers who were not spiritualists, it has seemed almost incredible that Doyle of all people should have

[1] Myers had been devoted to spiritualism for many years before the S.P.R. was founded. His friend Lady Battersea described him in her memoirs, "A poet when we first knew him, as the years went on he became an ardent Spiritualist, and one of the first members of the Society for Psychical Research" (*Reminiscences*, London, 1922, p. 205). Myers's experience was not dissimilar to that of Doyle "When, in February, 1869, an attack of pneumonia put his life in danger, Myers realised that he was not a Christian; and for the next few years he vacillated between complete agnosticism and a troubled half-belief. His doubts caused him great distress. He needed a religious belief more intensely perhaps than most men can readily understand." A. Gauld, *The Founders of Psychical Research* (London, 1968), p. 99.

[2] *Journal*, S.P.R., February, 1893, p. 17. Thirty-seven years later, a few months before his death, Doyle resigned in high dudgeon amidst some publicity. In January, 1930 he sent a circular letter, which included the text of his letter of resignation to the Chairman of the Council, to every Member and Associate of the S.P.R. He urged others to follow his example, and to transfer their allegiance to the British College of Psychic Science (*Journal*, S.P.R., March, 1930, pp. 45–52).

[3] *The New Revelation*, p. 38. Despite his normally remarkable memory, Doyle was sometimes oddly inaccurate in regard to dates and facts when writing upon psychic matters. Thus, in "Early Psychic Experiences" in *Pearson's Magazine* in March 1924 he quoted in the text a séance message received in General Drayson's house at what he described as "about this time (1886)" (p. 204). On the opposite page he reproduced photographically his own preserved notes of *the identical message* signed "Typical of the kind of message got in our private Circle in 1888. A.C.D." (p. 205).

been a believer in psychic phenomena. Writing of his public conversion in 1916, John Dickson Carr said with obvious bewilderment:

> "Did you mention Crookes, or Lodge, or Russel Wallace? These were honoured men of science, admittedly; but they corresponded to the Absent-Minded Professor of the comic paper, who tipped his wife sixpence and kissed the porter goodbye. They were secluded from life, entitled to such foibles. But Conan Doyle?
>
> This fellow had bowled W. G. Grace. He had bowled W. G. Grace: which, in America, corresponded to striking out Ty Cobb with three pitched balls. He could make a three-figure break at billiards, or hold his own against any amateur heavy-weight. He had created Sherlock Holmes. For a quarter of a century he had loomed thick-shouldered as the sturdy Briton, with no damned nonsense about him. What was wrong? What ailed the man?"[1]

It seems clear that what puzzled Carr so much was that a famous sportsman and man of the world could believe in psychic phenomena and accept the claims of spiritualism; that a vigorous, extroverted lover of adventure, fresh air and an open view across the Sussex Downs could become addicted to the semi-darkness of the séance room and to a faith that most reasonable men have considered to be little else but fraudulent superstition. Yet Doyle was by no means the only example of such a contradiction.

A curiously apt parallel is the case of a near contemporary of Doyle, Windham Thomas Wyndham Quin (1841–1926), the fourth Earl of Dunraven, whose letters (as Viscount Adare) to his father on the subject of spiritualism were printed for private circulation by the third Earl in 1869 as *Experiences in Spiritualism with Mr. D. D. Home*.[2] In his autobiography Adare said that his devotion to shooting and fishing began when he was a boy. He said, moreover, that the sea was his "master-passion". When he was twenty he already owned a disused Cardiff pilot-boat which he fitted out as a small yacht, and spent much time sailing along the Cornish and Devonshire coasts

[1] Carr, pp. 322–3.
[2] The case of Adare and the very odd circumstances surrounding the printing of a now exceedingly rare book are discussed in my *New Light on Old Ghosts* (London, 1965).

during his leaves from service as a cornet in the 1st Life Guards.[1]

In the Preface to the S.P.R. reprint of *Experiences in Spiritualism* he wrote with justification of his young manhood, "I loved sport and an active 'out-of-doors' life".[2] Jean Burton wrote of him:

> "The normal pursuits of Lord Adare, a thin, wiry, monocled, cheerfully extrovert young Guardsman in his early twenties, were sailing, horse-racing, big-game shooting, and anything that promised a dash of excitement."[3]

Adare's career as an internationally famous yachtsman, a hunter and a war correspondent (and in later life a man of public affairs) shows that these assessments of his personality were true. Yet for two years, 1867–9, from the age of twenty-six, Lord Adare willingly shared the sedentary, twilight life (and even the bed) of Daniel Dunglas Home (1838–1886), the Victorian physical medium, and wrote to his father, the third Earl, of "elongation", "levitation", "trances" and "spirits" as if they were matters of proven fact.

It is of great interest to know from the fourth Earl's autobiography that as a young man he had violently revolted, precisely as Doyle revolted, against his father's ardent Roman Catholicism. Like Doyle, Adare was educated by the Jesuits, and during his teaching in Rome was presented to Pope Pius IX. The result was identical in each case; defiance of family, the outright rejection of Roman Catholicism (other organised faiths going overboard simultaneously) and a consequent, inevitable religious vacuum into which spiritualism could and did intrude. Adare was to write in 1922:

> "The climax came when my father wanted me to go to the Roman Catholic College at Oscott, Birmingham. I refused. I had the only scene I ever had with a father I loved and respected; but I would not go . . . The inevitable consequence was indifference, hardening into disbelief in anything; and for the subsequent reaction spiritualism has something to say. Spiritualism—I mean spiritualism in its modern phase—has for many years been a subject of abuse, derišion, and controversy, but always of interest. Latterly, owing

---

[1] Earl of Dunraven, *Past Times and Pastimes* (2 vols., London, 1922), i, pp. 34–5.
[2] *Proceedings*, S.P.R., xxxv, Part 93, June, 1924, p. 23.
[3] *Heyday of a Wizard* (London, 1948), p. 191.

probably to the terrible losses which nearly every family in the country sustained during the war, interest in the subject has been intensified, and naturally my thoughts have reverted to the experiences I gained in studying the subject more than half a century ago."[1]

In parenthesis, we may notice that Adare, who married on 29 April, 1869, and more or less abandoned all participation in spiritualism for half a century, experienced a revival of interest due to the cataclysm of World War I, and as a result, under the persuasion of Sir Oliver Lodge, allowed the S.P.R. to reprint *Experiences in Spiritualism* in 1924. Doyle's reaction was not dissimilar. It was not (as has sometimes been suggested) the personal loss of his son, Captain Kingsley Conan Doyle, nor of his brother, Brigadier-General Innes Hay Doyle (who both died of pneumonia as a result of active service) that precipitated the last public phase of Doyle's devotion to spiritualism, starting in 1916. Doyle said that he had "many times refuted this clumsy lie".[2] Kingsley died only a fortnight before Armistice Day (Doyle was actually lecturing on spiritualism at Nottingham when the news reached him), while Innes's death did not take place until February, 1919, the year after *The New Revelation*, Doyle's first psychic book, was published. It was the impact of the horror of a world-wide disaster upon a sensitive and compassionate man that caused Doyle to write:

> "In the presence of an agonized world, hearing every day of the deaths of the flower of our race in the first promise of their unfulfilled youth, seeing around one the wives and mothers who had no clear conception whither their loved one had gone to, I seemed suddenly to see that this subject with which I had so long dallied was not merely a study of a force outside the rules of science, but that it was really something tremendous, a breaking down of the walls between two worlds, a direct undeniable message from beyond, a call of hope and of guidance to the human race at the time of its deepest affliction. The objective side of it ceased to interest, for having made up one's mind that it was true there was an end of the matter."[3]

[1] *Past Times and Pastimes*, pp. i, 7–10.
[2] *The History of Spiritualism* (London, 1926), ii. p. 224. The notion persisted after his death. "When his son was killed in the World War his belief in spiritualism came into full flower." (*The Evening News*, 11 July, 1930).
[3] *The New Revelation*, p. 49.

Doyle's statement in *The New Revelation* in 1918 that until 1916 he had merely "dallied" with spiritualism seems to me to be of great importance, as I hope to show. He confirmed it himself by his remark in 1927 in "THE PSYCHIC QUESTION AS I SEE IT", which I have already quoted, that prior to his public conversion his activity in spiritualism had been limited to "reading and occasional experiment". The first chapter of his *The New Revelation*, which he called "The Search", provides additional confirmation, since the experiences he described after he left Southsea in 1890 were limited indeed. He recorded nothing until shortly after he had joined the Society for Psychical Research, when he told of a visit to an allegedly haunted house at Charmouth in Dorset:

> "About this time I had an interesting experience, for I was one of three delegates sent by the Psychical Society to sit up in a haunted house. It was one of these poltergeist cases, where noises and foolish tricks had gone on for some years . . . Nothing sensational came of our journey, and yet it was not entirely barren."[1]

After the visit to Charmouth in 1893 or 1894, Doyle had only one experience to record in "The Search" in *The New Revelation* until he wrote (p. 48):

> "I have now traced my own evolution of thought up to the time of the War . . . I was culpably slow in throwing any small influence I may possess into the scale of truth. I might have drifted on for my whole life as a psychical researcher, showing a sympathetic, but more or less dilettante attitude towards the whole subject, as if we were arguing about some impersonal thing such as the existence of Atlantis or the Baconian controversy. But the War came, and when the War came it brought earnestness into all our souls and made us look more closely at our own beliefs and reassess their values."

---

[1] *The New Revelation*, pp. 42–3. In his article "Early Psychic Experiences" in *Pearson's Magazine*, March, 1924, he said that he visited the haunted house "in 1892 or 1893" with Frank Podmore and Dr. Sydney C. Scott of the S.P.R. In his last book, *The Edge of the Unknown* (London, 1930) Doyle again told the story, saying (p. 163) "I joined the Society for Psychical Research in 1893 or 1894 and must now be one of the oldest members. Shortly afterwards I was asked to form one of a small party to inspect a house at Charmouth. It was said to be haunted". If any report of the case was published by the S.P.R., I have been unable to trace it in the *Journal* or *Proceedings*, and it was evidently regarded as of small importance. The fact that Doyle published it so frequently suggests that his practical experience of investigation was limited indeed.

Doyle's single personal experience between the visit to Charmouth and the War, as recorded by him, was apparently with the materializing medium Frederick Foster Craddock, who was exposed in glaring fraud by the spiritualists themselves in 1906. After his account of the Charmouth case in *The New Revelation* (pp. 42–5) he wrote:

> "From this period until the time of the War I continued in the leisure hours of a very busy life to devote attention to this subject. I had experience of one series of séances with very amazing results, including several materializations seen in dim light. As the medium was detected in trickery shortly afterwards I wiped these off entirely as evidence . . . Up to the time of this incident I had never sat with a professional medium at all."[1]

Even if these records were not available to us, it is surely obvious to anyone acquainted with the facts of Doyle's full, varied and outstandingly successful life from 1887, that until he was approaching the age of sixty he could not conceivably have found the time to devote to any serious practical investigation of alleged psychic phenomena and the claims of spiritualism, nor is there any account of his having done so. His enormous literary output, including his creation of Sherlock Holmes, Brigadier Gerard and Professor Challenger and his magnificent historical novels, needs no emphasis, since it is documented by his seven biographers and his two bibliographers.

During the South African war of 1899–1902 Doyle acted as the senior physician at the Sir John Langman field hospital, and wrote not only *The Great Boer War* (1900), but his *The War in South Africa. Its Cause and Conduct* (1902), which was translated into twelve European languages. In this booklet, of which 100,000 copies were given away, Doyle justified England's war against the Boers and vindicated her conduct of the campaign, which had been widely and viciously traduced. He was knighted and appointed Deputy Lieutenant of Surrey in 1902 and received an LL.D. *honoris causa* from Edinburgh

---

[1] *The New Revelation*, pp. 45–6. The exposure of Craddock in the fraudulent impersonation of "spirit forms" by Lieut-Col. Mark Mayhew and Admiral W. Usborne Moore was reported in the spiritualist periodical *Light* of 24 March, 1906. The reports signed by these gentlemen were re-printed in the S.P.R. *Journal* of May and June, 1906.

University in 1905. At the age of 55, after unsuccessfully trying to enlist for service in the First World War, he published his booklet expounding the British cause, *To Arms* (1914), and founded a militia for national defence. His 6-volume *The British Campaign in France and Flanders* was published in 1916–19.

This was the man, too, who had been a physician (additionally trained as an eye-specialist), was an omnivorous reader, an indefatigable correspondent and a devoted family man. Politically conscious, Doyle supported tariff reform and Colonial preferance and stood, unsuccessfully, twice for Parliament. He advocated the Channel Tunnel, and for ten years was President of the Divorce Law Reform Union. He worked with E. D. Morel on the Congo Association, both speaking publicly and producing his book *The Crime of the Congo* (1909). He publicly championed the causes of George Edalji, Oscar Slater and Roger Casement.

Doyle was a formidable all-round amateur sportsman, and enjoyed the distinction of capturing the wicket of W. G. Grace in first-class cricket. He was one of the best amateur heavy-weight boxers of his day, and used his knowledge of pugilism in one of the finest of his historical novels *Rodney Stone* (1896). He reached the third round of the Amateur Billiards Champion-ship, drove as one of the British team in the Prince Henry race against Germany and introduced ski-ing into Switzerland. On the first page of his autobiography *Memories and Adventures* (1924) Doyle wrote, "I have had a life which, for variety and romance, could, I think, hardly be exceeded".

If it be accepted, on the basis of the facts of Doyle's life and his own published observations, that he announced his con-version to belief in psychic phenomena and in spiritualism as a religion in 1916 without having undertaken any serious investigation of the subject, then much becomes understandable. Miss Mercy Phillimore, the Secretary of the London Spiritualist Alliance from 1918 to 1952, naturally knew Doyle well, for he was the President. In 1959, the one-hundredth anniversary of Doyle's birth, Miss Phillimore contributed a long, appreciative essay, "SIR ARTHUR CONAN DOYLE. CHAMPION SPIRITUALIST", to the New York psychic journal *Tomorrow*.[1] She wrote of his conversion in 1916, "In one leap it led him past psychical

---

[1] Vol. 7, No. 4, Autumn, 1959, pp. 65–75.

research (where the weight of proof tacitly remains upon those who would establish survival) into the acceptance of the whole-hearted spiritualist". In my view this observation carries conviction. Doyle himself, as we have seen, conceded that until 1916 he had only "dallied" with spiritualism to the limited extent of "reading and occasional experiment", thus supporting Miss Phillimore's remark (p. 74) that there are no records of Doyle having made any personal researches of a scientific nature into alleged psychic phenomena and spiritualism prior to his conversion. Yet in *Light* in 1916 he wrote:

"We have reached a point where further proof is superfluous, and where the weight of disproof lies upon those who deny".

Doyle's "one leap", as Miss Phillimore aptly called it, into full and enthusiastic belief in 1916, after a necessarily superficial examination of the evidence, was yet again documented by him in 1918 in his first psychic book:

"When the War came . . . the objective side of it ceased to interest, for having made up one's mind that it was true, there was an end of the matter. The religious side of it was clearly of infinitely greater importance."[1]

Miss Phillimore wrote of this statement by Doyle, "The last line [sentence?] is of interest, as it seems to offer an explanation of the mystery of his alleged 'credulity' in his support of many controversial manifestations". In their sympathetic and admirably balanced book concerning Doyle and Harry Houdini, Bernard M. L. Ernst and Hereward Carrington said that Doyle's attitude at the spiritualist séances he attended after his conversion was, "I am in the presence of a new revelation from the Great Beyond; I must approach it in a spirit ·of reverence and prayer."[2] In the same book a letter to Houdini from Doyle is quoted, in which the latter wrote that spiritualism should "be approached not in the spirit of a detective approaching a suspect, but in that of a humble, religious soul, yearning for help and comfort".[3]

[1] *The New Revelation*, pp. 48–9. In an unpublished letter to Sir Oliver Lodge of 5 November, 1919, Doyle wrote, "I see it all from the religious angle, and so may drift away from the scientific".

[2] *Houdini and Conan Doyle. The Story of a Strange Friendship* (London, 1933), p. 29.　　　　　　　　　　　　　　　　　　　　　[3] *Ibid.*, p. 51.

Once converted to spiritualism as a religion in 1916, Doyle naturally sat with many mediums, never in a spirit of critical inquiry but entirely in the context of his advice to Houdini that I have already quoted. Miss Phillimore mildly observed in her essay in *Tomorrow* (p. 74):

"Many accounts are to be found of sittings he took after his acceptance of evidence for survival. Those accounts generally found favour among the 'converted', but were not favourably accepted by those psychical researchers whose object was to keep the investigation at a strictly scientific level".

All this suggests rather strongly that Harry Price's comment, already quoted on p. 96, that Doyle "made no pretence to studying phenomena from the scientific angle", was factually correct. His very qualities of large-heartedness and belief in the goodness of human nature, moreover, in the context of his crusading zeal as a propagandist of spiritualism, constituted his weakness. "Too honest himself", as Price wrote, in a passage I have already quoted, "he could not imagine his sympathetic credulity being imposed upon". Mrs. Muriel Hankey, for seven years Organising Secretary of the British College of Psychic Science (of which Doyle was President) and for a similar period Secretary and Principal of the London Spiritualist Alliance (of which Doyle was also President) wrote of him:

"Sir Arthur was a victim of his own fine character; [his] integral honesty could not believe people could act in this way . . . He may sometimes have pushed ahead in the psychic field without allowing himself adequate time to make detailed examination of matters which he felt he could take on trust."[1]

Once Doyle's attitude from 1916 to the end of his life is understood (and he himself declared it very simply when he said, "The objective side of it ceased to interest, for having made up one's mind that it was true there was an end of the matter"[2]), then we have the answer to the criticism so often levelled at Doyle (often by bewildered admirers) that "he used his skill as a writer to defend mediums against accusations of fraud".[3]

---

[1] *James Hewat McKenzie. Pioneer of Psychical Research* (London, 1963), p. 89.
[2] *The New Revelation*, p. 49.
[3] Martin Ebon, *They Knew the Unknown* (New York, 1971), p. 123.

Having once decided that he believed in these people, however dubious their reputations might appear to others, he was always ready to come to their rescue in print for precisely the same admirable reasons that he defended Edalji, Slater and Casement.

With some of the facts assembled, one cannot help suspecting that towards the end of his life Doyle, emotionally converted to enthusiastic belief in spiritualism as a religion, convinced himself that he had been scientifically investigating the subject closely and continuously since his Southsea days. Such self-deception in regard to the subject which had become the main interest and activity of his life would be quite natural, and we may think that it explains some of his published statements, which would otherwise be perplexing to those who were acquainted with the facts, and convincing to those who were not. In his autobiography, for example, he wrote:

"Finally, I have been constrained to devote my latter years to telling the world the final result of thirty-six years' study of the occult, and in endeavouring to make it realize the overwhelming importance of the question."[1]

As we have seen, Doyle's son perpetuated this notion in *The True Conan Doyle* by stating (the arithmetic was inaccurate) that his father "refused to pronounce any final judgment before he had devoted *thirty-three* years [Adrian Conan Doyle's italics] to his researches".

*   *   *

One circumstance that has to be remembered in regard to the adoption of spiritualism by men like Doyle was the period of religious ferment in England which had started in the latter half of the nineteenth century after the publication of *The Origin of Species* in 1859, the year of Doyle's birth. On the one hand was the agnosticism of many scientific men, whilst on the other was a Church divided against itself. Spiritualism, which was already flourishing in the United States before it spread to England, and claimed evidential proof for its teachings, seemed an attractive answer to many. One direct result was the

[1] *Memories*, p. 1. As the autobiography was first published in serial form in the *Strand* in 1923, Doyle's calculation was right, just as his son's was wrong; Doyle's conversion in 1916 took place 29 years after his introduction to the subject in 1887.

founding of the Society for Psychical Researsh in 1882 by Henry Sidgwick, Frederic W. H. Myers and William F. Barrett (after a conference convened by Barrett in the rooms of the British National Association of Spiritualists on 6 January, 1882), to be joined by men like Oliver Lodge, Alfred Russel Wallace and Edmund Gurney. Gurney, who became the Hon. Secretary of the Society, committed suicide in Brighton whilst in office,[1] five years before Doyle became a member.

In this connexion we may notice the coincidence that in their acceptance of the reality of psychic phenomena both Doyle and Adare were significantly influenced by what the latter stated to be the fact that spiritualism "has been critically investigated by the Society for Psychical Research and by other Associations. Many men eminent in the sphere of science have studied the subject".[2] Writing to Captain Stanbury on 10 July, 1913, Doyle remarked, "It is hard to put aside the experiences of trained observers like Crookes, Russel Wallace, etc. and say that it was a delusion. I believe that there was objective truth in their observations."[3] Five years later, in his first psychic book, Doyle repeated his confession that one of the most important factors in his belief in spiritualism was that if the "mature conclusions and careful investigations" of scientists like Crookes and Wallace endorsed it, then he "could not afford to dismiss it".[4] Only two years before his death he made the same point and quoted the same authorities in a public controversy with H. G. Wells in the Sunday press.[5] In an article "What Comes After Death", published in 1924, Doyle pressed this argument so far as to declare:

"One needs no experience oneself—though experience is always helpful. It is a question of evidence. If a man can carefully read such first-hand experiences as Crookes' 'Research upon Spiritualism' [sic], Crawford's two books upon physical phenomena,[6] and the

[1] The story of Gurney's life and death is told in my The Strange Case of Edmund Gurney (London, 1964).
[2] Experiences in Spiritualism (S.P.R. reprint), p. 21.
[3] Nordon, p. 155.   [4] The New Revelation, p. 22.
[5] "Why H. G. Wells is peeved", Sunday Express, 8 January, 1928.
[6] Dr. W. J. Crawford wrote three books about his experiences with the physical medium Kathleen Goligher and her family in Belfast. They were The Reality of Psychic Phenomena (London, 1916), Experiments in Psychical Science (London, 1919) and The Psychic Structures at the Goligher Circle (London, 1921), the last

chapters in Wallace's Autobiography which deal with the subject, and if a comparison of these documents does not convince him of external intelligence, then I claim that that man's mind is not well-balanced, and his logical sense is wanting."[1]

To many it will seem tragically ironic that Doyle, the creator of Sherlock Holmes and the amateur criminologist who solved the riddles of George Edalji and Oscar Slater, should fatally have attached so much importance to William Crookes's *Researches in the Phenomena of Spiritualism* (London, 1874), and have regarded it as an acceptable substitute for personal investigation. It was in this book that the mediumship of the notoriously fraudulent Florence Cook (together with her supposed materialization "Katie King") was endorsed by Crookes in circumstances so suspicious that most sensible persons, both at the time and today, have considered that Crookes's favourable reports (on one occasion embellished with verse filched from Byron's *Don Juan* without acknowledgement)[2] were dictated by Miss Cook's undisputed and by no means unavailable sexual attractions,[3] and not as a result of scientific inquiry, but a so-called investigation in which the names of the witnesses were concealed and only Crookes himself was allowed to enter the medium's "cabinet".[4] Crookes

being published after Crawford's death. Doubts were thrown upon Dr. Crawford's beliefs by Dr. E. E. Fournier d'Albe in his book, *The Goligher Circle* (London, 1922), in which he recorded that during a long series of sittings from May to August, 1921, he obtained almost no results. Dr. Crawford died by suicide on 31 July, 1920. It is fair to record that five days previously he wrote, "I have been struck down mentally. I was perfectly all right up to a few weeks ago. It is *not* the psychic work."

[1] *Pearson's Magazine*, April, 1924, p. 312.

[2] The plagiarism was unnoticed until I published it in 1962. It is therefore of great interest to read Dr. A. da Silva Mello's published remark two years earlier that Crookes "wrote verses throbbing with the love which had been inspired by the young girl whose beauty he considered to be indescribable" (*Mysteries and Realities of this World and the Next*, London, 1960, p. 394).

[3] Florence herself later confessed that she had been Crookes's mistress. In the D. D. Home collection at the S.P.R. is part of a letter written by Mr. J. C. Luxmoore, J.P., in which he revealed that Florence's husband, Captain E. Elgie Corner, had given Crookes "a very good thrashing, and in my opinion he richly deserved it". Crookes took out a summons for assault against Corner, but failed to appear at court and was ordered to pay the whole of the costs.

[4] The story of Crookes and Florence Cook has been told in my *The Spiritualists* (London, 1962), *Florence Cook and William Crookes. A Footnote to an Enquiry* (London, 1963) and *New Light on Old Ghosts* (London, 1965), and in Dr. E. J. Dingwall's *The Critics' Dilemma* (Crowhurst, 1966). Lady Williams-Ellis included an excellent short account of the affair in her *Darwin's Moon. A*

subsequently became involved with another fraudulent young medium of the period, Mary Rosina Showers. In his correspondence with D. D. Home (which the S.P.R. owns but has never published)[1] Crookes said that he was "getting the reputation of a Don Juan", and that the extent of the scandal over Miss Showers and himself was such that he felt that he must put the affair in the hands of his lawyer. In the event, as he wrote to Home later, he "agreed to let the matter drop", thus duplicating his ultimate prudent lack of action over the thrashing administered by Florence Cook's husband, Captain Corner. Of this imbroglio with Mary Showers Dr. E. J. Dingwall, acknowledged throughout the world as the leading authority on the history of spiritualism and psychical research, wrote:

> "We know from the evidence of Crookes's own letters that he was quite willing generally to conceal the fact that he had reason to suppose that Mary Showers was fraudulent and to share the secret with a few friends who connived at the plan. He remained silent when Mary was still giving her performances in a half drunken condition within a few miles of the S.P.R. headquarters. In my opinion he had good reasons for this attitude."[2]

Of Doyle's other authority, Alfred Russel Wallace (whose second forename is consistently misspelled by Professor Nordon throughout the whole of his *Conan Doyle*), the great naturalist's biographer, Lady Williams-Ellis, says of "the whole sordid business" of Crookes and Florence Cook that "it is certain that Wallace was among those who were influenced by Crookes's repeated private and public assertions that pretty Miss Cook

Biography of Alfred Russel Wallace (London, 1966) as did the late Simeon Edmunds in *Spiritualism: A Critical Survey* (London, 1966). Critical comments (in my opinion defamatory) in regard to Crookes's infatuation were made openly at the time, principally by the Rev. C. M. Davies in *Mystic London: or, Phases of Occult Life in the Metropolis* (London, 1875), by J. N. Maskelyne in *Modern Spiritualism* (London, 1876) and even by a convinced spiritualist, J. Enmore Jones, in the periodical *Medium and Daybreak* of 22 May, 1874.

[1] Some extracts relevant to the affair were printed on pp. 72 ff. of my *New Light on Old Ghosts*.

[2] *The Critics' Dilemma*, pp. 71–2. It may be thought that there is justification for Dr. Dingwall's comment that despite the distinctions bestowed upon Crookes very much later in life (he was knighted at the age of 65 and received the O.M. when he was 78) there can be little doubt that in his early forties he "was moving in a corrupt and shabby world and was sometimes keeping very dubious company" (*ibid.*, p. 39).

really went into trances and that, after this, spirit forms were really seen both by him and other sitters". Lady Williams-Ellis adds, in defence of Wallace's credulity in regard to spiritualism in general (which she admits) and to his attitude to Crookes's experiments with Miss Cook in particular, that "the deceptions and the motives that lay behind them were anyhow probably too bad to have been believed by the candid and benevolent Wallace".[1] If this kindly judgement is right, then it is reasonable to extend similar forgiveness to Doyle, who seems to have accepted everything that Crookes and Wallace wrote about spiritualism.

Wallace's credulity in psychic matters was traditional. He publicly stated, for example, his implicit belief in the infamous medium "Dr." W. F. Monck, who in 1876 was glaringly exposed in Huddersfield, Yorkshire, by an amateur conjurer, H. B. Lodge. The medium fled to an upstairs room and escaped through a window with the aid of sheets. Among his luggage were found the usual impedimenta of fraudulent mediumship, including "spirit hands", masks, muslin etc. together with a number of obscene letters from women with whom Monck had carried on intrigues under the cloak of spiritualism and the convenience of dark séances. Monck was arrested, tried and sentenced to three months' imprisonment (the maximum penalty) as a rogue and vagabond. When giving evidence on oath in the subsequent Colley v. Maskelyne libel case, in which the question of the genuineness or otherwise of Monck's mediumship was an ingredient, Wallace said that very few mediums had been caught in fraud, adding, of the Huddersfield exposure: "Monck was not caught in the act of trickery. Monck was a guest on the occasion, and a demand was made that he should be searched, and he departed through the window."[2] When an amateur conjurer, S. J. Davey, using the simplest of trickery, reproduced as an experiment some popular mediumistic effects and invited the "sitters" to describe what they had seen, Wallace refused to believe that Mr. Davey had obtained

---

[1] *Darwin's Moon*, p. 186. J. Marchant, in *Alfred Russel Wallace: Letters and Reminiscences* (London, 1916), remarked that Wallace had "unfailing confidence in the goodness of human nature".
[2] *The Times*, 27 April, 1907.

his results by conjuring, and accused him of being a medium.[1] In her wholly sympathetic biography of Wallace, Lady Williams-Ellis observes: "He had here a will to believe, so that over spiritualism he did not exercise the care in weighing evidence that he showed in his scientific work."[2] The same observation was true of Doyle. Even his friend and fellow-spiritualist, Sir Oliver Lodge (they were knighted on the same day in 1902), in an address to the London Spiritualist Alliance in October, 1931, said of Doyle, the late President, that he "lacked the wisdom of the serpent, but the goodness of his motives must be manifest to all". He added:

"His methods are not mine; he regarded himself as a missionary,[3] a trustee of a great truth which he felt bound to share with others."

It seems clear that on the subject of spiritualism Doyle, over-enthusiastic and always far too busy, was prepared to rely very greatly on the inquiries and judgment of others, which he all too readily accepted without reserve. On pp. viii–ix of the Preface of his *The History of Spiritualism* he said, "It was clear that such a work needed a great deal of research—far more than I in my overcrowded life could devote to it." He therefore used the services of W. Leslie Curnow, a spiritualist of very small means who was much interested in the history of the subject. Curnow wrote articles for the psychic journal *Two Worlds*, and reprinted some of them in a book, *The Physical Phenomena of Spiritualism. A Historical Survey*, published in Manchester in 1925. The extent of Curnow's responsibility for *The History of Spiritualism* (the unfortunate factual inaccuracy of which has never been in serious dispute) is demonstrated by Doyle's generous acknowledgment on p. ix of the Preface:

"I had originally expected no more than raw material, but [Curnow] has occasionally given me the finished article, of which I have gladly availed myself, altering it only to the extent of getting

[1] *Journal*, S.P.R., March, 1891, p. 43, and cf. Dr. Richard Hodgson, "Mr. Davey's Imitations by Conjuring of Phenomena sometimes attributed to Spirit Agency", *Proceedings*, S.P.R., 1892, viii, pp. 253–310.

[2] *Darwin's Moon*, p. 185.

[3] In a letter to J. Arthur Hill of 31 August, 1923, deprecating Doyle's idea to set up a Spiritualist Church in London, Lodge wrote, "I suppose it is a natural outcome of his missionary activity. I suppose he regards himself as a sort of Wesley or Whitefield" (*Letters from Sir Oliver Lodge. Compiled and Annotated by J. Arthur Hill*, London, 1932, p. 181).

my own personal point of view. I cannot admit too fully the loyal assistance which he has given me, and if I have not conjoined his name with my own on the title-page it is for reasons which he understands and in which he acquiesces."

I have tried to show in the preceding pages how the converging circumstances of Doyle's extraordinary life and personality allowed spiritualism to intrude, almost inevitably, into the religious vacuum which for a time had followed his abandonment of Roman Catholicism. These influences included the times in which he lived, the impact of the First World War on his extreme compassion and sensitivity, his enormous activity in his literary work and a dozen other spheres of enthusiasm, his veneration of Crookes and Wallace, his complete faith in the goodness and honesty of the human animal and his psychological need for a religion. I think it also true to say that the love of mystery and adventure that was an obvious ingredient in Doyle's personality would cause spiritualism to be extremely attractive to him. The late Adrian Conan Doyle, writing of his father, endorsed the remark of Sir Max Pemberton that "it was ever the bizarre and the daring that drew Conan Doyle as a filing is drawn to its magnet".[1] Dr. George Lawton, the author of the definitive psychological study of spiritualism, observed that his experience had taught him that "to be fascinated by the obscure and the unusual is especially symptomatic" of the potential believer in spiritualism.[2] One extremely relevant example cited by Lawton was the criminologist Cesare Lombroso, who became an ardent spiritualist. Lawton added, with great insight:

> "It is perfectly true, of course, that while the crude, magical aspects appeal to the ignorant and naïve, the extremely complex and technical side of spiritualism appeals to the cultivated, intelligent and, to a certain extent, sophisticated class."[3]

Lawton could have quoted another cogent example, that of Dr. Walter Franklin Prince, who was a President of the Society for Psychical Research. In his Presidential Address, delivered on 14 July, 1930, Dr. Prince said:

---

[1] *The True Conan Doyle*, p. 7.   [2] Lawton, *op. cit.*, p. 546.
[3] Lawton, *op. cit.*, p. viii.

"I . . . have one chief passion, the essaying the solution of puzzles, and one chief qualification, a lifetime of indefatigable practice. I speak, then, from the viewpoint of one who likes to tackle puzzles, and has from earliest recollection. All sorts of puzzles in boyhood, mechanical, mathematical, verbal. Later puzzles as to literary genuineness, the identity of handwriting, mooted points in history, etc. Then puzzles in psychology. And finally puzzles in psychical research . . . Such, in a nutshell, has been the story of my being drawn into psychical research."[1]

Another example is that of Dr. Richard Hodgson (1855–1905), who was one of the main pillars of the S.P.R. in its early years and a man of brilliant intellect and scholarly education. Like Doyle, he "gloried in fresh air and healthy exercise",[2] and died from a heart attack whilst playing a game of handball on 20 December, 1905.[3] As Dr. Alan Gauld has written, "One source of [Hodgson's] interest in psychical research was simply a love of puzzles, mysteries, mystifications and conjuring, in all of which he took a quite boyish delight."[4] In parenthesis, it is worthy of mention that Doyle's almost endearing quality of obstinacy in his defence of spiritualism was similar to that of Hodgson. J. G. Piddington could have been writing of Doyle when he said of Hodgson:

"Once his mind was made up he became constitutionally unable to appreciate another point of view, and his strong convictions were accompanied by an almost righteous indignation at the perversity of the other fellow . . . At bottom he was so firmly convinced that his own side was best that when it was worsted, or in danger of being worsted, he felt a sense of injury because the righteous were not inheriting the earth. The promise of this inheritance to the meek must have been to him the hardest of Hard Sayings. Yet if he played, or wrote, or talked for victory with excessive zeal, I do not believe for one moment that egotism was the cause. *He knew* that his side was in right, and his plain duty was to make that side prevail."[5]

[1] *Proceedings*, S.P.R., xxxix, Part 115, pp. 273–4.
[2] Alan Gauld, *The Founders of Psychical Research* (London, 1968), p. 202.
[3] "Through Mrs. Piper the spirits prophesied a long and healthy life for him. Soon afterwards he was dead" (Gauld, p. 337). Hodgson believed completely in the mediumship of Mrs. Leonore E. Piper.
[4] Gauld, p. 336.
[5] *Proceedings*, S.P.R., 1905–7, xix, pp. 365–6. Hesketh Pearson recorded in print Ernest Short's letter about Doyle: "My personal reaction was that this man took his spiritual experiences so seriously and was so profoundly convinced of their

Yet another example was Angelo J. Lewis, a barrister-at-law who, under the pseudonym of Professor Louis Hoffmann, wrote over thirty extremely successful books on conjuring, puzzles, hand-shadows, card-games, drawing-room amusements and even tricycling (at which Doyle was an adept), and was a member of the S.P.R. and a member of its committee on physical phenomena in the 1880s. Lewis became much interested in the alleged phenomena of spiritualism. After a long series of sittings with the slate-writing medium W. Eglinton in 1885, upon which he reported at length,[1] he expressed doubt at first whether trickery could wholly be responsible for Eglinton's results. He later stated, however, that this doubt had been "greatly shaken" by Mr. S. J. Davey's experimental proof that it was possible for a skilful conjurer "to produce, under the same external conditions, results of precisely the same kind and quality as those produced by the professed medium".[2] In 1889, relying (as Doyle had done) on the writings of William Crookes, Lewis said of the physical medium D. D. Home that it seemed possible that he possessed "some special power of producing motion, without contact, in inanimate objects".[3] On the other hand, there can be no doubt whatever from Lewis's published views that he never deviated from his conviction that the notorious medium "Dr." W. F. Monck was a complete fraud.[4]

Doyle never personally learnt the skills and secrets of conjuring, but his friendship and correspondence with Harry Houdini demonstrated his great interest in the subject.[5] Can we seriously doubt, moreover, that Doyle, whose boyhood hero had been Poe's Auguste Dupin, the first real detective of fiction, was, like Cesare Lombroso, Richard Hodgson and W. F. Prince, "drawn into" the puzzles of psychical research and spiritualism partially, if not wholly, for similar reasons? Can we doubt that

truth that argument or even discussion was impossible; one might just as well have argued with St. Theresa about her mystical experiences" (Pearson, p. 175).
[1] *Journal*, S.P.R., June, 1886, pp. 327–9, and August, 1886, pp. 362–75.
[2] *Proceedings*, S.P.R., iv, 1887, pp. 485–6.
[3] *Journal*, S.P.R., July, 1889, pp. 119–20.
[4] *Ibid.*, July, 1889, p. 120, and October, 1889, pp. 143–6.
[5] On 11 May, 1922, Doyle wrote to Houdini, "Just a line to say how much we enjoyed our short visit yesterday. I think what interested me most was the little 'trick' which you showed us in the cab" (*Houdini and Conan Doyle*, p. 143).

this man, who identified himself with Sherlock Holmes, did not at least partially share the psychological structure of his creation, who said to Watson, "Give me the most abstruse cryptogram, or the most intricate analysis, and I am in my own proper atmosphere".[1] On the other hand, it must be conceded that as late as 1927, when *The Case-Book of Sherlock Holmes* was published, Holmes expressed his views on occultism without ambiguity, as he had previously done in cases such as those of *The Hound of the Baskervilles* and *The Devil's Foot:*

> "But are we to give serious attention to such things? This Agency stands flat-footed upon the ground, and there it must remain. The world is big enough for us. No ghosts need apply."[2]

* * *

And so we return to Sherlock Holmes, and to the small problem posed by Doyle's literary creation being a consistently outspoken sceptic on the subject of occultism. In his essay "Conan Doyle: Sherlock Holmes's Alter Ego", already quoted, Martin Ebon observes that Holmes "looks, in retrospect, like an antidote to the occult, an oasis of reliable, materialistic order. There are no spirit rappings on the walls of his house in Baker Street".[3] This comment suggests interest in the view advanced by Sherman Yellen, once Mr. Ebon's editorial colleague on the staff of the quarterly magazines *Tomorrow* and the *International Journal of Parapsychology*, whose essay on Doyle in the latter periodical has already been quoted. Ebon reminds us that "Yellen makes the psychologically interesting assumption that Doyle retained lingering doubts about the validity of spiritualist doctrine and the wisdom of all-out devotion to it".[4]

Yellen's main argument in his essay, published in 1965, is based on the friendship that existed between Doyle and Harry Houdini, the illusionist, from 1920 to 1924,[5] admirably documented by B. M. L. Ernst and H. Carrington in their *Houdini and Conan Doyle*. Yellen wrote:

> "In Conan Doyle's need to convince and convert Houdini to Spiritualist truth one may read the story of Conan Doyle's efforts

[1] *The Sign of Four*, L., p. 144.   [2] *The Sussex Vampire*, S., p. 1179.
[3] Ebon, *op. cit.*, pp. 125–6.   [4] Ebon, *op. cit.*, p. 125.
[5] *Houdini and Conan Doyle*, pp. 85 and 208.

to resolve hidden doubts of his own—doubts which lingered after his announced conversion. Houdini, like Holmes, represented that side of himself which remained rooted in materialist philosophy. It was necessary to kill Holmes as it was later necessary to break with Houdini when his intransigence against Spiritualism challenged Conan Doyle's own beliefs too strongly."[1]

The idea that Doyle identified in Houdini, as in Holmes, the side of his own nature that was still materialistic, and therefore doubted the reality of the phenomena of spiritualism, is evidently quite seriously advanced by Yellen. He writes on the same page: "In the years of close friendship and correspondence between these two men [Doyle and Houdini] one can see the Holmes–Doyle relationship—with all its conflicts and attractions—played out in real life."[2]

The notion is an interesting one, but it fails to carry conviction because it is at variance with the facts. Doyle did not "kill" Holmes because the latter "represented that side of himself which remained rooted in materialist philosophy". Early in 1893, when he was finishing the second set of Sherlock Holmes stories for the *Strand* (published in book form as the *Memoirs* in 1894) he wrote to his mother on 6 April, 1893:

"I am in the middle of the last Holmes story [*The Final Problem*], after which the gentleman vanishes, never to return! I am weary of his name."

The idea of writing no more Holmes stories was not new. As early as 11 November, 1891, he had written to his mother to say that he was thinking of finishing with Holmes,[3] because this highly successful series was interfering with what he regarded as his serious literary work—his historical novels. On this earlier occasion, his mother had dissuaded him.

"After all, he *had* been well paid for those tales. On the other hand, he was almost ready to begin work on his Franco-Canadian book, tentatively called *The Refugees*. To write another half-a-dozen Holmes tales would be to put off everything he really wanted to do; and he chafed at the delay."[4]

---

[1] Yellen, *op. cit.*, p. 48. The assertion that Doyle was troubled by lingering doubts about spiritualism after his conversion is repeated two paragraphs later on the same page.
[2] Yellen, *op. cit.*, p. 48.   [3] Carr, p. 87.   [4] Carr, p. 86.

A passage in Doyle's autobiography confirms Carr's account:

"At last, after I had done two series of [Sherlock Holmes stories] I saw that I was in danger of having my hand forced, and of being entirely identified with what I regarded as a lower stratum of literary achievement. Therefore as a sign of my resolution I determined to end the life of my hero . . . I was amazed at the concern expressed by the public. They say that a man is never properly appreciated until he is dead, and the general protest against my summary execution of Holmes taught me how many and how numerous were his friends . . . I fear I was only too callous myself, and only glad to have a chance of opening out into new fields of imagination."[1]

Despite his new-found freedom from Baker Street, enabling him to concentrate on the historical novels and other literary work he considered to be of more importance than detective stories, Doyle ultimately revived Sherlock Holmes, and after *The Hound of the Baskervilles* and *The Return of Sherlock Holmes*, collections of stories continued to appear until 1927, three years before Doyle's death. In the Preface to *The Case-Book of Sherlock Holmes* he wrote:

"I had fully determined at the conclusion of *The Memoirs* to bring Holmes to an end, as I felt that my literary energies should not be directed too much into one channel. That pale, clear-cut face and loose-limbed figure were taking up an undue share of my imagination. I did the deed, but, fortunately, no coroner had pronounced upon the remains, and so, after a long interval, it was not difficult for me to respond to the flattering demand and to explain my rash act away. I have never regretted it, for I have not in actual practice found that these lighter sketches have prevented me from exploring and finding my limitations in such varied branches of literature as history, poetry, historical novels, psychic research, and the drama."

With all respect for those who take the opposite view, I would say that even to anyone who reads with care nothing but Doyle's autobiography, the bibliographies of his published work by Locke and Nordon, and John Dickson Carr's admirable *The Life of Sir Arthur Conan Doyle*, it must surely be clear that the last decade of the nineteenth century was a period of immense literary activity for Doyle, and a time when his actual

[1] *Memories*, p. 99.

participation in spiritualism was virtually non-existent. Doyle's own simple explanation for the hiatus of nearly eight years in his writing about Sherlock Holmes from December, 1893, when *The Final Problem* appeared in *The Strand*, to August, 1901, when the first episode of *The Hound of the Baskervilles* was published in the same magazine, is confirmed by the record of his literary output, his correspondence and the circumstances of his life. It follows, without any doubt in my opinion, that there is no evidence to support the idea that Holmes was "killed" in 1893 because he represented to Doyle "that side of himself which remained rooted in materialistic philosophy".[1]

It is, of course, possible that I have not understood Mr. Yellen aright, and that by the "killing" of Holmes by Doyle he is referring to a later period and to his apparent belief, already quoted, that the Holmes stories ceased for ever during the First World War, "which claimed Sherlock Holmes as its victim. After Verdun, there could be no easy return to Baker Street".[2] Whilst such an assumption would conveniently fit with the date of Doyle's conversion in 1916, it is unfortunately demolished by the fact that Doyle continued to publish Holmes stories for another eleven years.

In the broad sense, it cannot be denied that Mr. Yellen is right to say that Doyle broke off his friendship with Houdini when the latter's "intransigence against Spiritualism challenged Conan Doyle's own beliefs too strongly".[3] I do not think, however, that the matter need be complicated by the theory that in Houdini, Doyle saw a duplication of a side of his own nature that doubted the reality of psychic phenomena.

The relationship between Doyle and Houdini was described and thoroughly documented by correspondence between the two men by B. M. L. Ernst, a distinguished lawyer and an amateur conjurer, and Hereward Carrington, a well-known psychical researcher, in their joint book *Houdini and Conan Doyle. The Story of a Strange Friendship*, to which I have already referred. There can be no doubt that Doyle and Houdini held each other in the highest regard, as their large correspondence demonstrates. Ernst and Carrington wrote of them:

[1] Yellen, *op. cit.*, p. 48.   [2] Yellen, *op. cit.*, p. 42.
[3] Yellen, *op. cit.*, p. 48.

"They disagreed absolutely on almost every conceivable point connected with the subject [of spiritualism]. In the Press and on the public platform they launched vigorous campaigns against each other. Each man tried to convert the other to his views through propaganda and correspondence. Their minds remained as divergent as the poles.

Nevertheless each man had profound respect, admiration, almost affection for the other. They met, they discussed these topics, they disagreed more fundamentally than ever. Yet Houdini is constantly reiterating his friendship and esteem for Conan Doyle; and Doyle wrote, in one of his letters to Mrs. Houdini: 'He was a great master of his profession and, in some ways, the most remarkable man I have ever known'."[1]

In a memoranda book on 17 June, 1922, after a meeting with Doyle in Atlantic City, Houdini wrote of his friend:

"His voice and mannerisms are just as nice and sweet as any mortal I have ever been near. Lady Doyle told me that he has never spoken a cross word in his life. He is good-natured, very bright, but a monomaniac on the subject of Spiritualism. Being uninitiated in the world of mystery, never having been taught the artifices of conjuring, it was the simplest thing in the world for anyone to gain his confidence and hoodwink him."[2]

There is no doubt that Doyle was most anxious to convince Houdini of what he believed to be the truths of spiritualism, and of the evidence for survival. Because of his affection and respect for his friend, moreover, he was exceedingly patient in his efforts in this regard. Even after it became obvious that no agreement was possible, Doyle wrote to Houdini on 19 November, 1922:

"However, I don't propose to discuss this subject any more with you, for I consider that you have had your proofs and that the responsibility of accepting or rejecting is with you. And it *is* a very real and lasting responsibility. However, I leave it at that, for I have done my best to give you truth. I will, however, send you my little book on Hope, but that will be my last word on the subject. Meanwhile, there are lots of other subjects on which we can all meet in friendly converse."[3]

---

[1] *Houdini and Conan Doyle*, p. 16.   [2] *Ibid.*, p. 147.   [3] *Ibid.*, p. 172.

Houdini's reply of 15 December, 1922, demonstrated a similar sincere wish to retain Doyle's friendship:

> "I hold both Lady Doyle and yourself in the highest esteem. I know you treat this as a religion, but personally I cannot do so, for, up to the present time, and with all my experiences, I have never seen or heard anything that could really convert me. Trusting you will accept my letter in the same honest good faith and feeling as that in which it was written."[1]

I believe that the principal reason for the end of the friendship between these two remarkable men was Houdini's inability to accept as genuine a supposed communication from his dead mother through the automatic writing of Lady Doyle. It would be entirely natural for Doyle to regard this as casting doubt on his wife's mediumship, and therefore as a personal affront. At the time of the séance Houdini remained silent, but he later swore a long affidavit in which he said:

> "There was not the slightest idea of my having felt my mother's presence, and the [script] which follows I cannot possibly accept as having been written or inspired by the soul or spirit of my sweet mother."[2]

Mr. Yellen himself recorded this *contretemps*, apparently without attaching the same importance to it that I do:

> "Houdini had expressed doubts about the validity of scripts produced by Lady Doyle in her automatic writing which purported to come from his mother. He pointed out the inconsistency in the form and content of the message with his mother's background. Conan Doyle, a devoted husband, was offended by this insult to Lady Doyle's psychic talents."[3]

There is no doubt that Houdini was convinced of the complete sincerity and honesty of Sir Arthur and Lady Doyle. The Cross on the top of the script,[4] the fluent English of the message,[5] and some other circumstances, however, caused him to be certain that the script did not emanate from his dead mother

---

[1] *Houdini and Conan Doyle*, p. 173.   [2] *Houdini and Conan Doyle*, p. 175.
[3] Yellen, *op. cit.*, p. 47.   [4] Houdini's mother was a Jewish lady.
[5] In his sworn statement "The Truth regarding Spiritualistic Séance given to Houdini by Lady Doyle" Houdini said, "Although my mother had been in America for almost fifty years, she could not read, speak, or write English" (*Houdini and Conan Doyle*, p. 175.)

but from the subconscious mind of Lady Doyle, just as many other communications of this kind have been composed by persons of complete honesty, without any help from the supposed spirit world. At the séance itself Houdini evidently said nothing, not wishing to offend the valued friends who had spontaneously tried to provide this evidence. He could not resist the urge to publish his side of the matter later, however. It seems to me significant that in his final letter to Houdini of 26 February, 1924, Doyle referred to the séance, after answering a request by Houdini for some item of information, in very different terms from their earlier correspondence:

> "You probably want those extracts in order to twist them in some way against me or my cause, but what I say I say and I do not alter. All the world can quote . . . I read an interview you gave some American paper the other day, in which you said my wife gave you nothing striking when she wrote for you. When you met us, three days after the writing, in New York, you said: 'I have been walking on air ever since,' or words to that effect. I wonder how you reconcile your various utterances?"[1]

So ended the correspondence and the friendship. Houdini sent Doyle a note on 5 May, 1924, offering to present a copy of his book *A Magician Among the Spirits*, but it was not answered. As I have said, and have now tried to document, I believe that the reason for Doyle's breaking his friendship with Houdini was a very simple and human one, just as was his "killing" of Holmes in 1893, and that no complex psychological explanation need be considered.

*   *   *

The supposed puzzle of the contradictory scepticism of Sherlock Holmes, pointed out by John Dickson Carr, Sherman Yellen and Martin Ebon and others, already quoted, lends itself to examination. The four relevant stories, and the dates of their first publication in the *Strand*, are *The Cardboard Box* (January, 1893)[2], *The Hound of the Baskervilles* (August, 1901–April,

---

[1] *Houdini and Conan Doyle*, pp. 208–9.
[2] The demonstration of pseudo-mind-reading by Holmes in this story was transplanted by Doyle to *The Resident Patient* when *The Memoirs of Sherlock Holmes* was published in book form in 1894. *The Cardboard Box* was omitted from the volume.

1902), *The Devil's Foot* (December, 1910) and *The Sussex Vampire* (January, 1924). It will be seen that the first three were published before Doyle's conversion to spiritualism in 1916, so that in these cases no problem of contradiction needs to be resolved. The puzzle is therefore really confined to the sentences in *The Sussex Vampire*, already quoted:

> "This Agency stands flat-footed upon the ground, and there it must remain. The world is big enough for us. No ghosts need apply."[1]

This passage was repeated when *The Sussex Vampire* was included in the first book edition of *The Case-Book of Sherlock Holmes* in 1927. These sentences certainly read oddly, apparently coming as they did from Doyle almost concurrently with the publication of *The Land of Mist* in 1926, in which he used the famous characters of *The Lost World* to present the case for spiritualism in the form of a novel.

One's perplexity is not diminished by the fact that these sentences were a quite gratuitous comment by Holmes so far as the actual story of *The Sussex Vampire* was concerned, as the title itself indicates. Mr. Robert Ferguson (or "Big Bob Ferguson, the finest three-quarter Richmond ever had", as Watson recalled him from the days when Watson himself played for Blackheath)[2] had reason to believe that his wife (it was his second marriage) was drinking the blood of her own infant son. Holmes investigated the case, and discovered that Mrs. Ferguson had actually been saving the life of her child from an attempt to murder him on the part of Ferguson's jealous son by his first wife. This vicious and unbalanced youth of fifteen had deliberately pricked the neck of his small stepbrother with a poisoned arrow, forming part of a collection of Peruvian weapons decorating the hall of Ferguson's Sussex home. The horrified mother had sucked the poison from the wound, a courageous act of which her husband had seen only the conclusion, and which she had refused to explain for her

---

[1] *The Sussex Vampire*, S., p. 1179. I thought that these remarks by Holmes were appropriate to the contents of my *New Light on Old Ghosts* (London, 1965) and I quoted them on the title-page.
[2] *The Sussex Vampire*, S., pp. 1182–3.

husband's sake. Holmes solved the case, remarking that his prescription for the youthful would-be assassin would be a year at sea. It will be seen that ghosts played no part in *The Sussex Vampire*. Indeed, Holmes's fierce scepticism on the subject of vampirism, which forms no part of the beliefs of spiritualism so far as I am aware, was already sufficiently expressed for the purpose of the story in his comment to Watson a few sentences before his remark on the subject of ghosts:

> "Rubbish, Watson, rubbish! What have we to do with walking corpses who can only be held in their grave by stakes driven through their hearts? It's pure lunacy."[1]

It is not in dispute, as the plot of *The Sussex Vampire* demonstrates, that the twelve stories forming *The Case-Book of Sherlock Holmes*, which originally appeared spasmodically in the *Strand* from October, 1921 (*The Mazarin Stone*), to April, 1927 (*Shoscombe Old Place*), showed a marked falling-off from the standard of the earlier cases. The question we have to answer is whether we believe that these stories were actually written during these years of Doyle's immense labours in the cause of spiritualism. If we look at the surrounding circumstances, we can say at once that all the probabilities are against the answer being in the affirmative. Between 1921 and 1927, as we have seen, Doyle wrote no less than nine of his thirteen books on spiritualism, and additionally published his autobiography of over 400 pages in 1924. From 1917 to 1920 Doyle lectured on spiritualism in nearly every town of importance in the British Isles, visiting many of them more than once. In August 1920 he set off on his Australian tour, and by March, 1921 he was in Paris boldly lecturing in French on psychic matters.[2] In 1922 and again in 1923 he toured the United States speaking on spiritualism, concluding with a visit to Canada for the same purpose. His biographer wrote of him, and especially of his extreme preoccupations from the early twenties:

---

[1] *The Sussex Vampire*, S., p. 1179.
[2] *Memories*, p. 397. In an unpublished letter to Sir Oliver Lodge of 5 November, 1919, Doyle wrote, "I have done nearly 50 lectures to 100,000 people, and mean to make it 100. It is hard work, but when one sees a good object all comes easy. Anyhow, 'I can do no other'. "

"By the end of 1923 he had traversed fifty thousand miles and addressed nearly a quarter of a million people . . . Through the middle years of the decade, 1923 to 1926, even a stranger—to say nothing of the worried Jean [Lady Doyle], who tried to shield him as much as possible—could have seen his labours were growing too great. His correspondence, which in America had reached the figure of three hundred letters a day, was only one item of it."[1]

It seems safe to say that if the stories of *The Case-Book of Sherlock Holmes* (which even included stories first published in the years of the American tours) were written from 1921 onwards, they must have been written under extreme pressure as "psychic books and articles, some of the latter in the 'Strand', poured from the pen of the man who could not rest",[2] during the last decade of Doyle's life. Our legitimate doubts whether they were written at this time at all, however, become near certainty, when we read Doyle's reply (quoted by Carr) to a letter from the Editor of the *Strand* begging him to write on something of more popular appeal than spiritualism:

"I wish I could do as you wish but, as you know, my life is devoted to one end and at present I can't see any literature which would be of any use to you above the horizon. I can only write what comes to me."[3]

Would a man, writing like this and under the pressure of work and priorities we have seen, write a story much as *The Sussex Vampire* at the period in 1923 superficially suggested by its publication in the *Strand* in January, 1924?

It is of interest to recall John Dickson Carr's words about the last story in the collection *His Last Bow*, which gave the book its name. It was first published in the *Strand* of September, 1917 as "His Last Bow: The War Service of Sherlock Holmes". Carr wrote of it:

"Even without our private knowledge of the author's state of mind, we can feel in the texture of *His Last Bow* that it is more than another adventure of Sherlock Holmes. It was, as the author subtitled it, an 'epilogue'. It was to be, really and finally, *His Last Bow*."[4]

[1] Carr, p. 329.   [2] Carr, p. 329.   [3] Carr, p. 331.   [4] Carr, p. 315.

And again:

"It is the last thrill, the final drumbeat, the apotheosis of Sherlock Holmes. The whole series should have ended with *His Last Bow*, as the author formally and finally meant it to end."[1]

I believe this to be completely true. The action of *His Last Bow* took place on 2 August, 1914, Holmes having been summoned out of retirement by the Prime Minister himself two years previously to assume his disguise as Altamont, a period of work of great risk for Holmes, that was to result in the defeat of the German master-spy, Von Bork. 1914 was, of course, a much later date than any of the previous cases of Sherlock Holmes. It is therefore curious to look at the dates of the action of cases which formed the subsequent collection of *The Case-Book*, all of which were earlier than 1914.

One of the most important dates in any biographical account of Sherlock Holmes is that of his retirement from active practice in Baker Street to the Sussex Downs. This is fixed for us approximately by Watson's remark in *The Creeping Man*, "which formed one of the very last cases handled by Holmes before his retirement from practice". Watson gave the date of the start of the case as "one Sunday evening early in September of the year 1903".[2] Despite the fact that in *His Last Bow* Doyle had made Holmes "a tall, gaunt man of sixty",[3] who had retired from practice eleven years previously, in all but one of the cases subsequently published in *The Case-Book* collection, he and Watson are still in Baker Street. The single exception is *The Lion's Mane*, the action of which takes place near Holmes's "little Sussex home" in July, 1907.[4] The action of *The Veiled Lodger*, for example (in my view one of the weakest of all the stories, in which Watson admitted that there was little or no "opportunity of showing [Holmes's] curious gifts of instinct and observation") took place as early as 1896.[5] Others in which specific or inferential dates appear in the text are *The Retired Colourman* (1899)[6], *The Three Garridebs* (1902),[7] *The Illustrious Client* (1902)[8] and *The Blanched Soldier* (1903).[9]

[1] Carr, p. 317.
[2] *The Creeping Man*, S., p. 1244.
[3] *His Last Bow*, S., p. 1076.
[4] *The Lion's Mane*, S., pp. 1266–7.
[5] *The Veiled Lodger*, S., p. 1288.
[6] *The Retired Colourman*, S., p. 1320.
[7] *The Three Garridebs*, S., p. 1197.
[8] *The Illustrious Client*, S., p. 1089.
[9] *The Blanched Soldier*, S., p. 1118.

In earlier days Doyle set himself a very high standard in writing the Holmes stories. He said in his autobiography:

> "I was determined, now that I had no longer the excuse of absolute pecuniary pressure, never again to write anything which was not as good as I could possibly make it, and therefore I would not write a Holmes story without a worthy plot and without a problem which interested my own mind, for that is the first requisite before you can interest anyone else."[1]

In this connexion, it is of great interest to notice that we have evidence of at least two stories about Sherlock Holmes written by Doyle which he considered were too weak and fanciful for publication. One is referred to by Hesketh Pearson in *Conan Doyle: His Life and Art*:

> "Among his papers I discovered a *scenario* for an uncompleted tale which gives us a rough idea of the early stages of his work before he filled it out and pulled it together."[2]

The story (which takes place in the Baker Street days)[3] involves a murderer on stilts, who is induced to confess to his crime by a man employed by Holmes and Watson to impersonate the murdered man, "wizened body, grey shrivelled face, skull-cap, and all". This apparition, mounted on a pair of stilts, appears outside the murderer's window in the moonlight crying "As you came for me, I have come for you!" When Holmes and Watson rush upstairs the murderer, "mad with guilty terrors", clings to them and points to the window shrieking "Save me! My God! He has come for me as I came for him". After this dramatic scene, the murderer collapses and makes a complete confession. We may think that Doyle was right to allow this story to remain in the privacy of his drawer.

John Dickson Carr found another Holmes story, *The Man Who Was Wanted*, which Doyle had "rejected and put away". The action took place in 1895, and Watson's wife was still Mary Morstan. It concerned the disappearance of a man from ship-board, under the eyes of witnesses,[4] which reminds us perhaps of the single tantalising remark by Watson on the subject of "Mr. James Phillimore, who, stepping back into his

---

[1] *Memories*, p. 97. [2] Pearson, p. 93. [3] Pearson, pp. 93–5.
[4] Carr, p. 332.

own house to get his umbrella, was never more seen in this world".[1]

We are entitled to wonder, in the face of the evidence of these discarded tales, whether originally there were more of them, written in the years before Doyle's conversion to spiritualism in 1916, when he had the time and the inclination to write about Sherlock Holmes, but adhered to the earlier high standards he set himself. Were the stories ultimately published as the series from 1921 to 1927 in the *Strand*, and in book form as *The Case-Book* in 1927, included in the drawer of tales discarded as sub-standard by Doyle in earlier years? Certainly the plots of *The Blanched Soldier*, *The Mazarin Stone*, *The Sussex Vampire*, *The Creeping Man* and *The Veiled Lodger*, to mention five examples, may cause us to wonder, when we compare them with the early masterpieces that took the world by storm.

It may, of course, be urged that Doyle would be unlikely to change his mind over stories that he had originally considered to be below the standard of the earlier Holmes cases. I think that the answer to this is that in the nineteen-twenties his interest was entirely focused on spiritualism, and that Holmes had become unimportant. He was being importuned, moreover, by the Editor of the *Strand*, as his biographer records:

> "'More Holmes?' Greenough Smith had been inquiring. And again: 'I can only write what comes to me'."[2]

There was also the question of the large amount of money that Doyle felt it to be his duty to devote to the cause of spiritualism during this period, which included the cost of the publication of his psychic books, the upkeep of his Psychic Bookshop in Westminster, which ran at a substantial loss, and his open-handed support of every aspect of the movement. The total amount involved, as stated by Carr, surprised me, but Doyle's biographer had the testimony of the family at his disposal when he wrote:

> "In a matter of hard cash, which we can all understand, he devoted two hundred and fifty thousand pounds to promoting the cause of Spiritualism."[3]

[1] *Thor Bridge*, S., p. 1215.   [2] Carr, p. 332.   [3] Carr, p. 332.

In my view, Doyle would attach much more importance, in his state of mind at this time of his life, to the considerable flow of money (to be devoted, of course, to spiritualism) that would result from the publication of *The Case-Book of Sherlock Holmes*, than to earlier misgivings about the standard of the stories themselves.

For the investigator and the textual critic, there is some suggestive evidence connected with *The Mazarin Stone*, one of the stories in *The Case-Book* and first published in *The Strand* in October, 1921, which would support such a hypothesis. The same plot, which was weak in the extreme, and the same characters (with one all-important and significant change) had previously been used by Doyle in an unsuccessful play, *The Crown Diamond*. We are without any information regarding the date when this play was originally written, but it is not difficult to see some significance in the fact that Dr. Watson, who had been described by Doyle as an "elderly man with a grey moustache" in *His Last Bow* published in *The Strand* in September, 1917, should be addressed as "young man" in *The Crown Diamond*.[1] We may also notice that the villain of *The Crown Diamond* was Colonel Sebastian Moran, formerly Chief of Staff in Dr. Moriarty's great criminal organisation and 'the second most dangerous man in London".[2] In *The Empty House*, the action of which took place in the Spring of 1894,[3] Colonel Moran was already "an elderly man"[4] (although still "one of the best shots in the world"[5]), when he was arrested for the murder of the Hon. Ronald Adair.[6] It would therefore be curious, or so it seems to me, if Doyle had made Moran the principal character in a play written, say, a quarter of a century after Holmes had said of him to Watson in 1894, "Meanwhile, come what may, Colonel Moran will trouble us no more".[7]

There are some echoes of *The Empty House* in *The Crown Diamond*, although the plot of the latter is that of *The Mazarin Stone*. Moran, as in *The Empty House*, has an airgun as a

---

[1] A. Conan Doyle, *The Crown Diamond. An Evening with Sherlock Holmes. A Play in One Act* (privately printed by the Baskerette Press in 59 copies for subscription only. New York, 1958). This rare little volume is not paginated and the reference is to A7 verso.

[2] *The Empty House, S.*, pp. 580–1. [3] *Ibid.*, p. 559.
[4] *Ibid.*, p. 575. [5] *Ibid.*, p. 581. [6] *Ibid.*, p. 583.
[7] *Ibid., S.*, p. 583.

potential murder weapon,[1] whilst Holmes has for protection a dummy of himself in the window of the sitting-room in Baker Street which "may get a bullet through its beautiful waxen head at any moment".[2] In *The Crown Diamond* Holmes has a book, compiled by himself, in which the life of Colonel Moran is recorded, as in *The Empty House*.[3] From it he reads to Moran a list of his crimes:

> " 'You're all here, every action of your vile and dangerous life'. 'Damn you, Holmes! Don't go too far.' "[4]

The second of these offences is the murder of "young Arbuthnot" just before his intended exposure of Colonel Moran "for cheating at cards", which it will be recalled was his precise motive for shooting the Honourable Ronald Adair in *The Empty House*. Holmes's records of Colonel Moran's crimes in *The Crown Diamond* contain nothing later than 1892, moreover, the year of Moran's involvement in a train robbery on the Riviera and in a forged cheque drawn on the Crédit Lyonnais.[5] All this seems firmly to place *The Crown Diamond* in the early eighteen-nineties, and suggests that the play may well have been written about then, at the same period as *The Empty House*. The evidence suggests that it was put together, and temporarily discarded as sub-standard, before *The Empty House* was published and Colonel Moran's career brought to an end for good. It seems to me very suggestive that the picturesque character of the card-playing tiger-shooting master-criminal of *The Crown Diamond*, complete with his powerful air-gun and a wax dummy of Sherlock Holmes at which to shoot, was used in its entirety in *The Empty House*, and that the murdered "young Arbuthnot" of *The Crown Diamond* was undoubtedly a prototype of the Honorable Ronald Adair of *The Empty House*, murdered by Colonel Moran for precisely the same reason.

The history of *The Crown Diamond* is of great interest. On 11 July, 1947, it was announced in the press that the sons and daughters of Conan Doyle had discovered the manuscript, along with other memorabilia, in an old hat-box in the vaults of a bank

[3] *The Crown Diamond*, B1 recto.
[3] *The Empty House*, S., pp. 580–1.
[5] *The Crown Diamond*, B4 recto.
[2] *Ibid.*, B1 verso.
[4] *The Crown Diamond*, B4 recto.

in Crowborough, Sussex. It had been written by Doyle, without date, in a penny exercise book, which was later displayed at Item No. 54 at the Sherlock Holmes Exhibition in New York in 1952, where it was erroneously described as "a play in one act, by A. Conan Doyle . . . based on the short story *The Adventure of The Mazarin Stone*". James Montgomery, a formidable Baker Street critic, challenged this assumption a year later, as I do myself. Whilst observing that the plots were identical, he said that all the evidence indicated that the story was written after the play.[1] This cannot be anything but correct, for in fact the play was publicly performed before *The Mazarin Stone* was published in *The Strand*. It was given its first single performance at the Hippodrome, Bristol on 2 May, 1921. On 16 May, two weeks later, it was put on for a week at the London Coliseum. After one further week's trial at the same threatre on 29 August, 1921, it faded away for ever, so far as I am aware. There is no record of it being ever performed in America. For a play about Sherlock Holmes, it must be regarded as a total failure. In my view this was entirely to be expected on the basis of Doyle's original judgment of it. I believe that the only acceptable explanation of Doyle's actions in first putting on the previously discarded play in 1921, and then hastily adapting and publishing it as *The Mazarin Stone* in October of the same year, was an endeavour to make money (which *The Strand* was most anxious to pay)[2] to devote to the cause of spiritualism.

The Crown Diamond was privately published in 1958 through the devotion of a great Sherlockian, the late Edgar W. Smith, in 59 copies only, which were not offered for sale. He described it in his Foreword as "this unbelievably corny play", full of "gimcracks" and "pyrotechnics" and "naïve contrivings".[3]

[1] "Speculation in Diamonds", *Sherlock Holmes Journal*, i, No. 4, December, 1953.
[2] In an article about the closing down of the *Strand*, "A Magazine Dies—and a Fifty-Year Secret Comes Out" in the *Daily Express* of 14 December, 1949, it was stated, "When Sherlock Holmes first appeared in the new sixpenny Strand Magazine in 1891, Conan Doyle was paid £35 a story. By the time the last of the Holmes adventures appeared in 1927, the Strand was paying more than £800 for the British rights alone." This fact was revealed by the Editor, Macdonald Hastings.
[3] *The Crown Diamond*, A3 recto and A4 recto. Smith justified the printing of the play by his remark in the Foreword, "We must not cavil at the amateurish quality of this play which has been rescued at last from limbo . . . It is, after all, about Sherlock Holmes." I treasure my copy for the same reason.

Smith himself remarked that the suggestion that the play was adapted from *The Mazarin Stone* was in conflict with all the probabilities, and that it was almost certainly the fact that the story was adapted from the play.[1] I agree, and I consider that there is evidence in the two texts which amounts to proof.

The Mazarin Stone (significantly in my view) was the first of the collection of stories contained in *The Case-Book of Sherlock Holmes*. As a play, it had hastily (I suggest) been taken from the drawer of discarded material and a license for its performance obtained from the Lord Chamberlain on 22 April, 1921, only just in time for it to be rehearsed and performed, it may be thought, in Bristol on 2 May, 1921. It is reasonable to suppose that this precipitate decision was the reason why Doyle did nothing to correct the glaring error, caused (I suggest) by the passage of time since the play was first written and discarded, of the presence of Colonel Sebastian Moran as the villain, when this already elderly gentleman in 1894 had been disposed of by Doyle over a quarter of a century earlier. When the play was converted into *The Mazarin Stone* a few months later (for publication in *The Strand* of October, 1921, with alterations so minimal as to make the task virtually a secretarial one) this inconsistency was evidently noticed. The single alteration was that the master criminal was changed from Colonel Moran to Count Negretto Sylvius. It is interesting to notice that Holmes's list of the Count's crimes ended in 1892, exactly as had those of Colonel Moran, with which they were identical.

If it is considered that there is acceptable evidence to show that *The Mazarin Stone* was not a new story written by Doyle in 1921, but had been salvaged from the past, then it becomes much easier also to believe that Doyle did not write *The Sussex Vampire* in 1923, at a frantically busy time, seven years after he had declared that for the rest of his life he would devote his pen and his voice entirely to the teaching of spiritualism. It will be seen that I believe that there is a general case to be answered for *The Sussex Vampire*, like *The Mazarin Stone* and the other stories of *The Case-Book of Sherlock Holmes*, having been written a good many years before Doyle handed them over to the *Strand* for publication in the nineteen-twenties. I think that the

[1] *The Crown Diamond*, A3 verso.

converging circumstantial evidence in this regard is hard to set aside. If this is right, and *The Sussex Vampire* was indeed written before Doyle's conversion to spiritualism in 1916, then the apparent inconsistency of Holmes's remark about ghosts is resolved.

I do not consider that there is any acceptable evidence to show, as Sherman Yellen has asserted, that Doyle had "hidden doubts of his own about the truth of spiritualism—doubts which lingered after his announced conversion".[1] Carr wrote of him:

> "For the cause of psychic religion he gave his heart, his worldly possessions, and finally his life."[2]

Doyle's last book, *The Edge of the Unknown*, was published in June, 1930, the month before his death. In the short Preface he wrote:

> "We who believe in the psychic revelation, and who appreciate that a perception of these things is of the utmost importance, certainly have hurled ourselves against the obstinacy of our time. Possibly we have allowed some of our lives to be gnawed away in what, for the moment, seemed a vain and thankless quest. Only the future can show whether the sacrifice was worth it. Personally I think that it was. Among the various chords which are struck in this little book there may be some to which the mind of the reader will respond, and which may entice him also in the search for the Holy Grail."[3]

---

[1] Yellen, *op. cit.*, p. 48. The assertion that Doyle in his last years had "lingering doubts" about spiritualism is repeated by Yellen on the same page.

[2] Carr, p. 338.

[3] *The Edge of the Unknown*, p. v. The most interesting (and by far the longest) chapter in the book is "The Riddle of Houdini". Read in conjunction with *Houdini and Conan Doyle*, by Ernst and Carrington, and the late Fr. Herbert Thurston's essay "The Case of Doyle v. Houdini" (*The Month*, August, 1930, pp. 97–109), this chapter completes the account of the relationship between the famous magician and the creator of Sherlock Holmes. A significant chapter is "Some Curious Personal Experiences", which underlines the paucity of Doyle's personal contact with psychical research and spiritualism prior to his conversion in 1916. He included (as always) the story of his visit to the supposedly haunted house at Charmouth, which he had already told in *The New Revelation* and in "Early Psychic Experiences" in *Pearson's Magazine*. Of the listed mediums with which he said he had "experimented" the majority (twenty-two) were encountered during his lecture tours in America, Canada, Australasia, South Africa, France, Denmark and Sweden, all of which took place in the nineteen-twenties. Of the mediums Doyle "sampled" at home and which he listed, I think that only Craddock

Doyle may have been right about spiritualism, or (as I believe) he may have been wrong about it, but there can be no doubt about his complete belief in it. As his last illness began he wrote to B. M. L. Ernst:

"I write this in bed, as I have broken down badly, and have developed Angina Pectoris. So there is just a chance that I may talk it all over with Houdini himself before very long.[1] I view the prospect with perfect equanimity. That is one thing that psychic knowledge does. It removes all fear of the future."[2]

In the end, his complete belief in spiritualism hastened his death:

"One of the last acts of his life had been to struggle up to London, against all Jean's and his doctors' pleading, so that he might see the Home Secretary about the law persecuting spiritualistic mediums. But the old horse had drawn its heavy load too far; it would take the road no more in this world."[3]

A few days later, Doyle was dead. John Dickson Carr wrote that it was a scene more like a quiet garden-party than a funeral-service when Doyle was buried in the grounds of Windlesham near the garden hut which he had so often used as a study:

"Word had spread that they did not wish mourning; there was little sign of it in the vast crowd who attended on that sunlit day of July 11th, 1930. But they missed him. And the world missed him. People at home, people in far places, saw pictures and remembered dreams when they heard he was gone. When the telegrams arrived, and the special train to carry the flowers, it seemed that all on earth remembered him."[4]

came within the pre-conversion period. Doyle himself described all these mediums as being "of the last twenty years", but his isolated experience with Craddock was some years before the First World War, as I have shown.

[1] Houdini had died four years earlier.
[2] *Houdini and Conan Doyle*, p. 17.
[3] Carr, pp. 336–7.   [4] Carr, p. 338.

INDEX OF CASES

INDEX OF NAMES, PLACES AND PUBLICATIONS